MORRIS VENDEN

Wonderful Words of Life

New pictures of grace
in the parables of Jesus

D1531986

MORRIS VENDEN

Wonderful Words of Life

New pictures of grace in the parables of Jesus

PACIFIC PRESS® PUBLISHING ASSOCIATION
Nampa, Idaho
Oshawa, Ontario, Canada
www.PacificPress.com

Designed by Michelle C. Petz

Cover image (ten virgins) copyright © 2003 Goodsalt.com

Unless otherwise noted, all quotations from Scripture are from
the New International Version. (NIV) the Holy Bible, New International
Version, copyright © 1973, 1978, 1984 by the International Bible Society. Used
by permission of Zondervan Bible Publishers.

Additional copies of this book are available by calling toll free
1-800-765-6955 or visiting www.AdventistBookCenter.com

Library of Congress Cataloging-in-Publication Data:

Venden, Morris L.

Wonderful words of life : new pictures of grace
in the parables of Jesus / Morris Venden.

p. cm.

ISBN: 0-8163-2008-X

1. Jesus Christ—Parables. I. Title.

BT375.3.V46 2004

226'.06—dc22   2003066418

04 05 06 07 08 • 5 4 3 2 1

Table of Contents

Chapter 1

New Wine, Old Bottles

About a hundred years ago I went off to study at La Sierra College to be a minister, a cowboy, or a jazz drummer. They were offering only one of the three so I took that one. My father said, "It costs me $25 a month to keep you at home, so I'll send that to you and you can work for the rest of it." Attending La Sierra cost a thousand dollars a year at that time. Someone told me the other day that it is now about $18,000. Ouch!

Well, I tried hard to make it, including trying to stay within the guys' minimum food charge per month, which was $20. One month I stayed within the girls' minimum, $16. They said, "You might as well come down to the cafeteria and get something to make up the difference." So I went down and came back to the room with four gallon jugs of cider—new cider. It became very popular down at my end of the hall, especially after a few days had gone by and we began to discover the difference between new cider and old cider.

Jesus told a story about new wine and old bottles. I've wanted to write about this story for a long time, but I've always hesitated. I never felt ready. I still don't feel ready. But I thought I might as well go for it—maybe I could learn something in the process.

The story is found in Luke 5:36-39:

He told them this parable: "No one tears a patch from a new garment and sews it on an old one. If he does, he will have torn the new garment, and the patch from the new will not match the old. And no one pours new wine into old wineskins. If he does, the new wine will burst the skins, the wine will run out and the wineskins will be ruined. No, new wine must be poured into new wineskins. And no one after drinking old wine wants the new, for he says, 'The old is better.' "

What is Jesus saying here? I propose that there are some great treasures all through this parable that need to be found. And we need the Holy Spirit to guide us.

Three of the four Gospel writers included this parable in their books. Each adds a little different dimension to it. One of the main points that Matthew and Mark brought up but Luke didn't is that if you put new cloth on an old garment, the tear is made worse. This suggests that the old garment already has a tear in it—a rent, a fault, a problem. Another point is that if you put new wine into old wineskins, the wine will burst the wineskins, and both the wine and the wineskins will be ruined; they will perish (see Matthew 9:16, 17; Mark 2:21, 22). And in Luke 5, the passage we started with, the new does not agree with the old. New wine must be put in new bottles so they both are preserved. Then Luke makes this little addition: He says that some people say the old is better, "Don't give us the new."

What does the wine in this parable represent?

Keith Miller wrote a book several years ago called *The Taste of New Wine*. It became a bestseller. He also wrote a book called *The Second Touch*. That book deeply impressed H. M. S. Richards; he preached about it at camp meetings. Keith Miller was trying to reveal very honestly and openly his own experience in being a so-so Christian and then discovering the new wine. The new wine is the message of Jesus, the gospel in *all* its aspects. This new wine, the gospel, centers on the Cross, which suggests the blood of Jesus: "a fountain filled with blood drawn from Immanuel's veins, and sinners plunged beneath that flood, lose all their guilty stains."

So, the new wine—let us underscore this right at the start—is the gospel. May I remind you that it is the full gospel, not just half the gospel or part of the gospel. And it centers on Jesus and the Cross and His blood, which is able to free us not only from the guilt of sin but also from the power of sin. This is the new wine.

What about the old bottles? Well, let's go back to the introduction to this parable (which was a takeoff from what John the Baptist had said in introducing Jesus; see John 3:29):

> They said to him [Jesus], "John's disciples often fast and pray, and so do the disciples of the Pharisees, but yours go on eating and drinking." Jesus answered, "Can you make the guests of the bridegroom fast while he is with them? But the time will come when the bridegroom will be taken from them; in those days they will fast" (Luke 5:33-35).

What, then, is the setting? These people were questioning Jesus as a prophet. And perhaps one of the things they were questioning was that He was happy.

Do you think Jesus was happy? Or was He always sad? If Jesus was always sad, why would little children crowd around Him? The last I checked, Jesus was happy. And John the Baptist was happy. Do you know what he said when he introduced Jesus? The people asked him if he was the Christ or if he was the prophet. He said, "I'm not the Christ. I'm sent before Him." And then he said, "The bride belongs to the bridegroom. The friend who attends the bridegroom waits and listens for him, and is full of joy when he hears the bridegroom's voice. That joy is mine, and it is now complete" (John 3:29).

So, John the Baptist, who is considered a shouting, pulpit-pounding preacher who got after people for their sins, was also a joyful man. And Jesus apparently demonstrated that you can have joyful holiness. April Ousler, in her book on the parables of Jesus, says that the fact that Jesus was joyful was one of the things that caused the Pharisees and the other somber leaders of those days to be upset.

What else had happened just before Jesus talked about the wine and the bottles? Well, just before this, the paralytic had been let down through the roof there in Capernaum, and he went rejoicing on his way. Jesus had already healed many, many people. Then He made the mistake of calling Matthew from the publican's chair to follow Him. At this juncture Jesus had already chosen four disciples: Andrew, Peter, James, and John. Then came number five, Matthew. This was a big mistake. The minute Jesus said, "Follow Me," Matthew left his publican's booth and followed Jesus. As a result he was so joyful that he threw a party. He had a feast. And guess who was there? Jesus and His first four disciples. Guess who else was there? Scribes and Pharisees and those who were in the spy ring already looking to get Him. They said, basically, "Elijah and John the Baptist didn't go to parties. Your disciples aren't fasting. Is this the way to be holy?" Then Jesus came in with the bridegroom pitch and demonstrated, in spite of their concern, that it is possible to be holy and joyful at the same time. Maybe that is one of the reasons we enjoy having a music celebration. The angels apparently enjoy singing His praises as well. So, this is the setting.

TOO PROUD TO ACCEPT THE GIFT

This parable was first brought up to my attention in 1988 when Debbie Anfenson-Vance wrote an article for the Review and Herald during that centennial year of the momentous 1888 General Conference session. The basic thrust of her article—which became a classic, at least in my book—is that our problem is that we are too proud to accept the gift. Accepting the gift, for proud people, is like trying to take new wine and put it into old bottles. We can't stretch far enough. We have trouble accepting gifts. We have trouble accepting the fact that salvation is totally a gift.

To begin with, we have trouble accepting the fact that the forgiveness of our sin is totally a gift—that we don't have to do anything in terms of penance or trying to make up for our sins, that we can accept His forgiveness totally as a gift. And then we have trouble accepting that His *power* is totally a gift. We keep hanging on to this old idea that you've got to do something yourself. "God helps those who help themselves." Try hard, and God will help you with what you can't do. *"Cooperation"!* We keep sounding that from the housetop. *"Cooperation"* . . . No, the only cooperation that God wants from us is to let Him do it.

So, we have trouble accepting all of the gifts that God offers. And we think that we are good anyway. We don't see the significance of giving up on ourselves and becoming new bottles or new wineskins or new garments so the wine and the bottles and the cloth and the patches will be compatible. We don't realize that we are lost among the ninety and nine. We don't realize that we are the prodigal son's brother. We don't realize that we are chronically late to our full-time jobs in the vineyard even though we work the twelve-hour day, or almost. We don't realize that we need the gift of salvation just as much as the lost sheep, just as much as the prodigal son, and just as much as the twelve-hour or the one-hour workers. This was the thrust of Debbie's article. It caused some of us to pause and think.

When I began to search around for help on this parable I discovered that the great preachers have done very little on it. It seems to be almost ignored. Charles Spurgeon had nothing to say on it. I've got fifty-five thick volumes of Spurgeon, so I said, "C'mon, Spurge, why don't you deal with this one?" Then I went to the Bible commentaries that our church published several years ago. Basically there is one page: Volume 5, page 1088. What's the thrust there? That Jesus, when He was looking for followers, when He was looking for disciples, kicked the dust off of His feet at Jerusalem. He did try the temple first. It didn't work. So He went to the seashore, the smelly seashore, where He could find new bottles for His new wine. In other words, it's very difficult to present the gospel to people who are hardened in traditional religion.

Have times changed much? Bill Hybels realized that they haven't. When he set about starting a church, he determined that he would not start with old bottles. He would not begin with old garments. He would start brand new—fresh.

Hybels knocked on people's doors and asked, "Do you go to church?"

"Yes."

"Wonderful, thank you. Have a nice day." On to the next door.

"Do you go to church?"

"No."

"Do you mind telling me why?"

Hybels kept a record of the whys. After hundreds of visits he compiled the records and found out the reasons why people don't go to church. "The church is always asking for money." "There's a trap in the foyer; they're going to get you." "The church is not relevant to our needs." "The church is sloppy in its programming." And so he started a little church—a small group of people way out of Chicago—based upon trying to meet the objections of these people who said they didn't go to church. The basic point is that he started from scratch. And people began to come and listen. He tried to talk to their needs. He planned the programs a year in advance, including what the people on the program were going to wear. He had it planned down to the second—a challenge to the media, if you please. He wasn't going to let the media upstage the good news of salvation in terms of careful presentation and all the rest of it.

There has been many a modern approach to the needs of our country based on this same idea. Go to a dark county. Go to a place where they haven't heard. Why should anyone hear the gospel twice before everyone has heard it once? Find some new bottles. Find some new garments. Find some smelly disciples down by the lake who are not too proud to accept the gift, who won't think that they are good and who will accept the salvation offered.

Well, I tried looking around a little more and discovered that we should remember that what was called new wine was not new wine. It was old wine—old in the sense that it had been heard before and it was true before. It is the same story that we heard twenty-five years ago. It's an old, old story. But it looks new. It looks new when you compare it with traditional religion, when you compare it with forms and ceremonies and routine. The relationship approach looks new when people are hooked on the behavior approach in religion and are hooked on going through the ceremonies and trying to save themselves by their own merit and their own works. It's like new wine in old bottles. The interesting thing is that in the symbolism the new wine bursts the old bottles. They're stretched out of shape. The wine is lost, spilled. And that's scary. Study it, neighbor. Take a look at it.

STEVEN'S STORY

I'll never forget a story I read about Steven. He lived in St. Louis. His twenty-one years had been hard on him. His arms were scarred from the needle, and his wrist scarred from the knife. His pride was his fist and his weakness was his girl.

Steven's initial response to love was beautiful. As the story of Jesus was unfolded before him, his hardened face would soften and his dark eyes would dance. He wanted to change. But his girlfriend would have none of it. Oh, she would listen politely and would be very sweet. But her heart was gripped by darkness. Any changes Steven made would be quickly squelched as she maneuvered him back into his old habits. She was the last thing standing between him and the kingdom. Those witnessing to him begged him to leave her. He was trying to put new wine into an old wineskin. He wrestled for days, trying to decide what to do. Finally, he reached the conclusion: He couldn't leave her. The last time those who were working with Steven saw him, he wept uncontrollably. They held big, tough, macho Steven in their arms and wept with him. The prophecy of Jesus was true. When His new wine was put into an old wineskin, it was lost.

Do you have any wineskins that need to be thrown out? Look closely in your closet. These skins come in all sizes. Maybe yours is an old indulgence: food, clothes, sex, gossip, profanity, or possibly, like Steven, an old relationship. No friendship or romance is worth your soul. Repentance means change, and change is needed because you cannot put new life into an old lifestyle.

These things Jesus was talking about are scary things. As I read this encounter with someone who apparently wanted the new way, I thought about how impossible it is to understand the kingdom of heaven until we are born again. Jesus said it: Unless you are born again, you cannot see the kingdom of God (see John 3:3-8). We usually think that the "kingdom of God" means heaven. Well, yes. But the word *see* also includes being able to understand the kingdom of heaven.

So, the new wine, the gospel, is not going to go very deep or very far until the new birth has taken place. Let me suggest that new birth is one of the greatest needs in the church today.

The new wine can be applied in terms of the individual, the one-soul audience—Nicodemus or Steven. The new wine and the old wineskins, or the old bottles, can also be applied to the family. What happens when new wine pours into a family that has been mediocre in terms of God and faith and spiritual things? Something begins to stretch. Something begins to burst. So you have one member of the family drinking the new wine of the gospel, and the other member of the family, like Steven's girlfriend, fighting, resisting, and going the other direction. There are families today that have experienced divorce because the shaking time has arrived and two lukewarm people go opposite directions: One becomes cold and the other hot. In fact, this splitting of families because of the shaking is on the rise, and before this shaking is over it will have made a great impact within the church. If you are in unity in your home in terms of the new wine, then thank the Lord and praise His name.

You can also have the new wine in the old bottles in terms of the church. Watch it when the great message of the gospel is presented to a church that is steeped in tradition or is a victim of form and ceremony or that is used to pop psychology and current issues and trying to deal with each other's "authentic selfhoods." Watch it! Something begins to stretch. Sometimes something bursts. And like some of us were told years ago, if you really get into the gospel, there will be battle scars. Yes, let's remember that Jesus wasn't referring to the world. He wasn't referring to the heathen—the Romans or the Greeks. He was referring to the church, the chosen people, when He spoke about wine bottles bursting.

What about the denomination? What happens when the new wine comes into a denomination? Not a bad thing to investigate or even take a look at history. In fact, I would like to take a look at history right now for a moment—case histories of new wine and old bottles. Let's start with Moses and the Exodus. We could go back a lot further than that. We could go back to Cain and Abel. But let's take a look at some of the great movements in which people were victims of the do-it-yourself, depending-on-your-own-resources religion. Again and again God tried to teach those people lessons of faith and of dependence upon Him.

Moses had new wine, and the old bottles were stretched and broken again and again. And patiently, God went through the process of trying to deal with these people year after year, decade after decade, century after century. His patience was awesome as He tried to teach them to be new bottles that could hold the new wine.

Come to the time of Jesus. His basic message was too much for the old wineskins. They couldn't handle it. In the end, the wineskins burst. Jesus had to walk away from those people and say, "Your house is left to you desolate" (Matthew 23:38).

Of course, the difference between the old and the new is demonstrated among His own followers too. Take a look at the great Reformation. What happened there? Luther bombed a gigantic system of ceremonies, rituals, penance, and merit. His message shook the system to its very foundations. It was new wine, and things began to burst in every direction. And some of the followers of Luther and millions of martyrs proved that when the new wine and the old bottles meet, the bottles burst and the wine is lost. The wine was spilled as the blood of thousands of martyrs was spilled.

NEW WINE IN OUR DAY

Coming down to our own day: We have within our own church history some classic examples of the new wine and the old bottles meeting. In 1888 the church resisted Jones and Waggoner and a few other voices. The *church* rebelled. Some of our church historians don't seem to agree. But during that period the church went into the wilderness to wander with the people of old. Those who were presenting the new wine left. The wine was spilled. The wine was wasted, and so it goes to this very day.

In 1958, which was seventy years later, some of us became interested in this "new wine" and began to try to teach it and to preach it. It seemed like we had been in captivity and seventy years was long enough. We began to consult with some of the old bottles and some of the old garments. I remember one of our world leaders telling me, after I explained to him my understanding of the gospel and righteousness by faith, "That's right. It's the truth, but don't preach it. You'll get into trouble."

One of my classmates at school had come out from spiritualism. At one time he had his own private devil in his house, and he and his wife would communicate with the spirits on a regular basis. One night he came to a series of meetings that my father was holding in Fresno. It was the first meeting he attended, and it happened to be called "The Mark of the Beast." He was startled. He cornered my father after the meeting and said, "I want to know more about this." My dad recognized that he was new and tried to be delicate with him. But this young man said to him, "You don't have to beat around the bush with me. Tell it to me straight." So, my father told him, and he was baptized.

He came to La Sierra and studied to be a minister. He was an older student, but he was sharp. Our major professor, Dr. Heppenstahl, told us one day that he was the sharpest one in the class. He said he had never seen anyone who could grasp the points and get the message so quickly and so thoroughly. Thank you very much, Dr. Heppenstahl; that really made our day!

Later, this young man began his ministry. He visited people who were victims of the old garments and the old bottles, people who were in trouble, whose lives were falling apart. And he asked them, "How long has it been since you've read your Bible?"

"Well, I used to, but I don't anymore."

"Have you ever read the book *The Desire of Ages*?"

"Well, no, I haven't."

"What about *Steps to Christ*? Have you looked at that?"

"No, I haven't."

And this young man, who was the sharpest of them all, got discouraged very quickly and left the ministry—because, he said, "These people aren't real. They're not serious with God. I'm not going to waste my time talking with people like these. They're fakes."

Old bottles. Old garments. Going through the motions. Second-, third-, fourth-generation church members, victims of religiosity. We have battle scars in the church. Glacier View is one of them. Someone had challenged some of our teachings. He happened to be an expert on presenting the gospel of justification. Some of us learned a lot about justification from him. The problem was he had only half the gospel. But he had that half, and he presented it. The church tried to deal with it. But in the process the bottles burst. The wine was spilled, and the voice was heard no more within our church. This has happened again and again.

So, what does this parable mean to us today?

First of all, by way of conclusion, I would like to remind you what this parable does *not* mean in terms of applications that some people have made from it. This parable does not mean that we should go out and get drunk with the drunkard. Jesus went out and ate with winebibbers and sinners, but He did not go out and get drunk with the drunkard. He did not go out to be like them. He went out to fellowship with them, to show them heaven's love, and to try and win them. There's a big difference.

This parable does not mean that we should go out and throw all our beliefs, our doctrines, our rules and standards and regulations, to the wind and say we are only interested in the new wine. Not at all. This parable does not allow for several different kinds of Adventists, for instance.

I would like to remind you that there are only two kinds of Adventists. There are only two kinds of Baptists, only two kinds of Methodists, only two kinds of people anywhere in the world: those who know Jesus and those who don't. That's it. And the only Adventist who will be saved, and the only Baptist who will be saved, and the only Methodist who will be saved, is the one who knows Jesus. We don't have different levels and different kinds of bottles and garments and wineskins, all of whom are going to be saved. There is only one gospel, and there is only one experience with

Jesus. It's very interesting to note that the experience with Jesus makes people pretty much the same the world over in terms of what they look like and how they act.

This parable does not mean that we can scrap the twenty-seven points of doctrine in favor of the new wine. Not at all. There are those among us today who champion that cause. "Oh, let's get rid of these rusty old twenty-seven points of doctrine." What we are way overdue on is seeing the new wine in *every* doctrine; seeing how the new wine, the full gospel, fits in every doctrine—not doing away with those doctrines, as some would have us do.

The other day someone noticed that I am concerned about the future of this church—and I am. How could I not be concerned that some would lead this church down the road to its own death? Yes, I am concerned. Some of us are praying diligently that God will help in the leadership of this church.

You ask, "Who are they? Give us some names." I'm not interested in telling you who they are. But I will tell what they are and what they do. People who tell jokes about the end time could lead this church to its death. People who talk more against the church than they do about Jesus will lead this church to its death. People who are leaders in our church and who are loose on Sabbath keeping could lead this church to its death. People who are leaders and who can easily take the Lord's name in vain could lead this church to its death. People who want a nondoctrinal witness of nothing more than "love everybody" could lead this church to its death. People who are soft on the inspired writings, the greatest gift to our church in these last hundred years, could lead this church to its death. People who make fun of vegetarianism, which was God's idea in the first place, could lead this church to its death. People who think that dress and adornment are not important issues could lead this church to its death. People whose standards and lifestyle are influenced by the crowd could lead this church to its death.

"Oh," you say, "aren't you nitpicking?" No, because these are symptoms. These are symptoms of those who are not serious with God. If I can easily take the Lord's name in vain in my slang language, I'm not serious with God or I'm not thinking. I have forgotten the third commandment: "Thou shalt not take the name of the Lord thy God in vain" (Exodus 20:7, KJV).

So, we're not looking at an array of nitpicking, legalistic points. What we're saying is that church leaders who are not converted and are demonstrating the unconverted life could lead this church to its death. Please pray, please pray, that God will help us as families, as a local church, as a denomination, to be new bottles and new garments, so that as the new wine continues to flow from Immanuel's veins, it will not be wasted.

Chapter 2

Plucking Out Your Eye

If you are considering gouging out your eye or cutting off your hand or cutting off your foot, you'd better let someone else do it. Someone else might know how to do it right.

Jesus uses some strong language in Matthew 5:29, 30. I'm going to call this passage a parable even though it isn't usually classified as one. This "parable" with its strong language shows up three times in the Gospels, twice in Matthew and once in Mark. It is Jesus' counsel to those who are getting serious with God, who want to be more than simply second-, third-, or fourth-generation church members. This is about those who are interested in getting serious about eternal life, who aren't settling for just a formal, routine religious experience.

Jesus said:

If your right eye causes you to sin, gouge it out and throw it away. It is better for you to lose one part of your body than for your whole body to be thrown into hell. And if your right hand causes you to sin, cut it off and throw it away. It is better for you to lose one part of your body than for your whole body to go into hell (Matthew 5:29, 30).

Jesus taught rather freely about hell, and so can we as we think about the options available to us. The issue in this passage is eternal life. And Jesus is obviously digging deeper than just a few short years on this planet Earth.

This passage is often overlooked. It sounds a little gory. It sounds a little tough. Just what exactly did Jesus mean? Well, to find some answers, I tried out the commentary that our church published several years ago. I came up with an old line that has been around a long time. I found disunity in our commentary's discussion of this passage. Let me show you. Here is the familiar line, for those of us who are overdosed with behavior-type religion: "He who refuses to see, hear, taste, smell, or touch that which is suggestive of sin, has gone far toward avoiding sinful thoughts."[1] So, some of our young people, after going through our school system, came up with a religion that is called, "Touch not, taste not, handle not." "By the plucking out of the eye or the cutting off of the hand, Christ figuratively speaks of the resolute action that should be taken by the will in order to guard against evil."[2] I tried that—until I discovered it doesn't work. You "guard the avenues of the soul, control your thoughts"—right?

This reminds me of the story of the Indian fakir who gave out a recipe for a pot of gold. He had you put in all of the ingredients and stir it over a fire. Then came the last instruction on the recipe: "And don't think of the red-tailed monkey, or it will ruin the pot of gold." Right! He made a lot of money on his recipe, and nobody ever got the gold either. That's because, of course, when you try *not* to think of the red-tailed monkey, you think of the red-tailed mon-key. "He who refuses to see, hear, taste, smell, or touch that which is suggestive of sin, has gone far toward avoiding sinful thoughts"? This is behaviorism's red-tailed monkey.

Well, the author of this passage in the commentary made the mistake of including an inspired comment that is just the oppo-site, as I see it: Christ lived a sinless life because "there was in Him nothing that responded to Satan's sophistry."[3] Do you see the dif-ference? Christ lived the sinless life because "there was in Him noth-ing that *responded.*" He didn't have to take resolute action of the will against evil because evil held nothing that attracted Him. That is precisely God's goal for us. But it still involves plucking out the eye and cutting off the hand. We will notice that it also involves cutting off the foot.

As we take a look at this parable, it is important that we review the settings in which it occurs in the three different places where it appears. The first occurrence, in Matthew 5, is in the middle of a section on lust. It is saying that the way to control lust is by pluck-ing out the eye. There have been some people, perhaps among the less informed, who were so sincere in their desire to live the right life that they actually did gouge out their eyes. They were trying to control their sinful thoughts. And they discovered, to their cha-grin, that it goes much deeper than that. There have been some who, in ignorance, cut off their hands or tried to avoid the world of sin by similar literal measures. But Jesus is talking about some-thing that is far deeper.

The second time this parable shows up is in Matthew 18:8, 9, where Jesus was talking about offending others. In the King James Version, verse 8 begins with the word *wherefore,* which means that what follows is related to something that went before. Looking back at verse 7, you'll notice that it has to do with offending the little ones, offending other people, or offending those who are young in faith, perhaps:

> If your hand or your foot causes you to sin, cut it off and throw it away. It is better for you to enter life maimed or crippled than to have two hands or two feet and be thrown into eternal fire. And if your eye causes you to sin, gouge it out and throw it away. It is better for you to enter life with one eye than to have two eyes and be thrown into the fire of hell.

DON'T OFFEND OTHERS

Then Jesus continues the theme introduced in the setting: "See that you do not look down on one of these little ones" (verse 10). So, here we have the appeal to live such a life that we don't offend someone else: perhaps the six-year-olds, or perhaps the new in faith as well. The apostle Paul emphasized this (see Romans 14:21). So, the setting here is: Don't offend others. It will be better for you to pluck out your eye and cut off your hand or foot than to offend others and cause them to stumble or be discouraged.

How am I going to accomplish this? What does it mean to pluck out the eye and cut off the hand?

The third passage, which is found in Mark 9:42-47, picks up the same setting—that of offending others. It is a little longer passage, and it throws in the foot as well:

> If anyone causes one of these little ones who believe in me to sin, it would be better for him to be thrown into the sea with a large millstone tied around his neck. If your hand causes you to sin, cut it off. It is better for you to enter

life maimed than with two hands to go into hell, where the fire never goes out. And if your foot causes you to sin, cut it off. It is better for you to enter life crippled than to have two feet and be thrown into hell. And if your eye causes you to sin, pluck it out. It is better for you to enter the kingdom of God with one eye than to have two eyes and be thrown into hell.

Well, here you have it—Jesus' strong language. What is He getting at here?

We are familiar with this kind of approach when dealing with health and life on this planet. We are familiar with going through major surgery in order to preserve life a little longer. We do it because it is good for us even though it means amputation or mutilation and ending up maimed. We are familiar with this approach to preserving life.

I became familiar with it in the home where I grew up when we discovered that Mother had cancer. The day came when we decided to go to the surgeon. I can still feel the knots in my stomach that I felt when the doctors came out from the surgery with the news that Mother's case was bad and that they were proceeding with major radical surgery. The pathologist gave her one chance in five hundred. I went to the restroom there in the Loma Linda Medical Center and began pounding on the wall and praying to God in behalf of my mother. Well, forty years later she died of something else at age ninety-one. Those forty years were good for us even though she had to go through them "maimed." I remember how I felt when she told me one day that sometimes she would look into the mirror and say, "Well, Jesus, if You were willing to go through what You did for me, I guess I should be able to put up with this without complaining."

So, some of us have been through this. We've seen it. We do it for life here on this earth, which has to do with three-score years and ten, because we take life seriously. What is life worth? Those facing capital punishment appeal for life. They go to another court even though they'll live in jail a life that is restricted and halt and maimed. Somewhere on the whole scenario we have to go into this issue of the choice between life and death. Are we anxious to consider eternal life with the same kind of seriousness? Or does this somehow fade away into the dim distance rather than the reality of here and now? Perhaps that's one of the reasons for asking God to help us think seriously concerning *now*.

Well, there are those who say, "If Jesus is not talking about the physical gouging out or cutting off—if instead this is a parable, then what is this parable about?" It is a parable about sacrifice. It is a parable about surrender. Please notice that this has to do with giving up on ourselves.

As I was reading a book called *Thoughts From the Mount of Blessing*, which is a commentary on the Beatitudes, the following statement really got my attention:

> God's purpose is not merely to deliver from the suffering that is the inevitable result of sin, but to save from sin itself. . . . In order for us to reach this high ideal, that which causes the soul to stumble must be sacrificed. It is through the will that sin retains its hold upon us. The surrender of the will is represented as plucking out the eye or cutting off the hand. Often it seems to us that to surrender the will to God is to consent to go through life maimed or crippled. But it is better, says Christ, for self to be maimed, wounded, crippled, if thus you may enter into life. That which you look upon as disaster is the door to highest benefit.[4]

This passage explains the spiritual meaning of the surrender of our life to God. It is called "the surrender of the will," which is represented by plucking out the eye or cutting off the hand.

Well, what is the will? Sometimes we say things like "he has—" "she has—" or "this little one has—a stubborn will." I was confused on this. I read a book called *Steps to Christ* years ago, and it described me. I was surprised that it knew me so well. It says,

> You desire to give yourself to Him, but you are weak in moral power, in slavery to doubt, and controlled by the habits of your life of sin. Your promises and resolutions are like ropes of sand. You cannot control your thoughts, your impulses, your affections. The knowledge of your broken promises and forfeited pledges weakens your confidence in your own sincerity, and causes you to feel that God cannot accept you.[5]

Thank you. How did the author know me that well?

"But," this book says, "you need not despair. What you need to understand is the true force of the will."

"Oh," I said. "That's my problem. I don't have enough force to my will." So I began to develop a more forceful will.

Have you ever been there? Have you ever tried that? We do it with diets, don't we? I have a book that stares at me from above the refrigerator. It's titled *How to Eat More and Weigh Less*. My, that sounds good! We go for it. But I'm going to turn it around the other way and say that it doesn't work.

WILL—NOT WILLPOWER

Then what do we mean by "will"? I thought it was willpower. But I found out that *Steps to Christ* is not talking about the willpower—not at all. It is talking about the will.

You mean there's a difference?

Yes, my *will* is my power to choose. My *willpower* is the power to do what I choose. *Willpower* we call "backbone," "grit," "determination." People from South Dakota have it. They have the power to do what they choose. *Will* is the power to choose; *willpower* is the power to do. I was confusing willpower with will. And to my surprise, the author defined it in the very next sentence: "You need not despair. What you need to understand is the true force of the will. This is the governing power in the nature of man, the power of decision or of choice."

So I reread the passage, substituting the words *power of choice* every time I found the word *will*. Notice how it reads and how this page was way ahead of its time: "*The power of choice* God has given to mankind. It is theirs to exercise." Toward what? "You cannot change your heart. You cannot of yourself give to God its affections. But you can choose to serve Him." In other words, you can choose to become His servant. A servant is controlled by the master. "You can give Him your *power of choice.*" You mean, I'm supposed to *give away* my power of choice? Yes. "He will then work in you to choose and to do according to His pleasure." You mean God will both choose and do in my life, if I will choose to turn my will, *my power of choice,* over to Him? Yes.

Is this biblical? Yes, Philippians 2:13 says, "It is God who works in you to *will* and to act according to his good purpose" (emphasis supplied).

But let's continue with *Steps to Christ:* "Thus your whole nature will be brought under the control of the Spirit of Christ; your affections will be centered upon Him, your thoughts will be in harmony with Him. . . . Through the right exercise of the *power of choice* an entire change may be made in your life. By *yielding up* your *power of choice*—" We're supposed to do that? We're invited to do that? Yes. "By yielding up your *power of choice* to Christ, you ally yourself with the power that is above all principalities and powers. You will have strength from above to hold you steadfast. And thus through constant surrender—" This is not just a one-time deal. This is a constant stance—"through constant surrender to God, you will be enabled to live the new life, even the life of faith."[6]

This came as a real shocker. It does away with the traditional approach of using your will and willpower to do what is right and not do what is wrong. That traditional approach is behavior theology and behavior religion, and it has led many people to become backsliders. But in this parable Jesus was talking about relationship theology, the relationship of the servant to the Master, being under the control of the Master. Except in this case it is *not* an abject slavery, such as we are used to in our world. It is a slavery of choice in which we invite God to take control of our life, just like we'd invite a surgeon to take control of our body. And if we are willing to go that far with a few short years here, why not go the next step into eternity?

People get worried though. They say they're afraid that God will take away our personality or individuality. No, He doesn't. The stubborn Dutchman will still remain a stubborn Dutchman—only instead of being stubborn for self, he'll be stubborn for God and His cause. That's what the apostle Paul became, as you recall. No, no—it is God who made us who we are. Can't we trust Him, then, for our personality and our individuality? Yes! He knows what makes us tick, and He doesn't invite us to gouge out our eyes and to cut off our hands and feet. He invites us to let Him do it—to surrender our will.

I guess it was about twenty or so years ago that I found myself in the geriatrics ward, or at least that's what it looked like. That's a strange place for a young buck to be. I was having cataract surgery on one of my eyes. I thought one had to have white hair and arthritis in order to do that. But there I was, in with the old folks, and the doctor plucked out my eye. I'm glad the doctor did it. I'm sure glad I didn't try doing it myself. He plucked out that part of my eye—that lens that was all fogged up. And I found out some years later, when I made plans to have the other eye done, that a small, foldable, intraocular lens is inserted through a small—less than 3mm—incision and unfolded in place of the natural lens. I couldn't believe it.

My doctor was so nervous—he was frightened to death about doing the operation because he knows me, and he gets nervous with people he knows. He said, "If I mess up, number one, I would want to die. And number two, I would need to die." I was so amused by his nervousness that I thought maybe during the surgery I could go, "Boo!" and have a little fun. But I decided I'd better not try that. I'm glad I have a doctor who takes his work that seriously.

Since those two operations, things have been a lot better. They were good for me. But first I needed to go to the doctor, and I needed to surrender to him and let him do it. And he did it right. You too have done it, and you have relatives who have done it. You understand this process. So, c'mon, neighbor! Why not use this with God? This decision has to do with eternity—with as many years of life as there are grains of sand in the seashore and more. Why can't we take God seriously?

So, I'm invited to surrender my will. "I surrender!" I say. It sounds easy, doesn't it? It's not that easy. If it was nothing more than words, some of us would have done it a long time ago. Then how is it done?

The same author whom I quoted earlier also said, "No man can empty himself of self. We can only consent for Christ to accomplish the work."[7] Now we're getting down to the bottom line, the nitty-gritty, the basics. All we ever do is consent for Him to do it.

So, if we say, "OK, I consent," is it done? No, because now we're getting into the basics of relationship theology. I choose to come into close relationship with the heavenly Physician, and this is the way I consent for Him to do the work. If I consent to take the first hour of my day alone with God, for instance, He's going to gouge out my eye. He's going to do surgery on my foot and my hand. In other words, He's going to lead me to surrender my will. Surrender is symbolized by the cross. "I have been crucified with Christ and I no longer live, but Christ lives in me," Paul says in Galatians 2:20. We cannot crucify ourselves anymore than we can do eye surgery on ourselves. He takes us there. Someone else has to crucify us. Crucifixion, the plucking out of the eye, the cutting off of the foot—even the yoke—are all symbols of the same thing: self-surrender, which we cannot do for ourselves. The closest we can come to doing it is to consent to come into a meaningful relationship with Him day by day. Then He will do it.

So, if I choose to spend quality time alone with Jesus day by day, He's going to take my will. And if I'm afraid that this will leave me maimed and halt, I probably won't do it. And that may be why many of us don't.

NOT SALVATION BY GRACE

After pastoring a church for eight years, I wondered if I could ever get the nerve to ask the congregation to level with me and tell me in some kind of survey or poll if my ministry had made any difference. Maybe it was idle curiosity, I don't know. I wondered if they had picked up that our whole goal for those eight years had been to try and help people enter into a daily relationship with Jesus. That's all. You say, "I thought the main message was that we were saved by grace?" No, there is no such thing as salvation by grace. It is always salvation by grace *through faith*. And faith is where *we* get into the picture. Living by faith begins when day by day we begin spending that precious hour in meaningful fellowship with God. That is the goal—for us to consent to spend as much time with God as we do eating our meals. And if we do, the surrender of the will is going to take place. It's a given. He will take us there, and, in the process, completely transform our lives, get us away from our sins and give us power for witness and outreach.

Will we be maimed and crippled? Maybe. But if we are, it will be good for us.

Jacob was his name. You remember him. He had a problem. He was a borderline, if not outright, liar. After he got finished with outright, he remained borderline. And for twenty years he was a careful maneuverer and planner and manipulator. He knew how to get things done. Who needs God when you can manipulate? Then came the big crisis in his life by the Brook Jabbok. He got in a fight with Jesus, and he fought most of the night. Then, at dawn, it dawned on him. At the breaking of the day he realized that he had been doing this for twenty years. He thought he had been fighting his own battles when in reality he had been fighting Jesus for twenty years. Yes, that is the problem. The way we fight Jesus is by fighting our own battles. And we always lose, one way or another, even though we think we win.

This was the crisis that brought about the big change in Jacob's life. After that night he never had the same problems again. He came back from the Brook Jabbok the next morning, and someone in the camp said, "Who is that coming?"

Someone else said, "Jacob."

"No! That's not Jacob. This man is limping."

"Yes, it is Jacob. He's limping because he's been with the Lord."

"Oh!" you say. "People don't limp when they've been with the Lord." Sometimes they do! Paul did. Others did. But it was good for them, because, as Paul wrote in 2 Corinthians 12:10, "For Christ's sake, I delight in weaknesses, in insults, in hardships, in persecutions, in difficulties. For when I am weak, then I am strong."

There are some of you who are limping because you have been with the Lord, and you can appreciate stories like that of Fannie Crosby, and songs like "He washed my eyes with tears"—why?—"that I might see" and "the broken heart I had was good for me." The question is, am I interested in getting serious with God—as serious as I am with the doctors—and trusting Him at least as much as I do the doctors? Can I do that? Can I trust Him?

As I was looking up material on this subject I ran across this famous little quotation: "One sin cherished is sufficient to work the degradation of the character and to mislead others." That triggered the relationship-theology definition of cherished sin. I used to think it was something I like to do that's wrong. No, no, no. Cherished sin is choosing to remain away from Jesus day by day and substituting something else in place of that relationship, including things like feverishly working for the church. If I do not have time to consent for God to do His work in my life day by day, that is cherished sin. That is the relationship definition of cherished sin. Here's how it works in practical terms: A particular issue shows up in my life, and I think, *Hey, I like this!* And I'm afraid that if I get with God, He's going to "gouge out my eye" and ruin my lifestyle. So I stay away from God and cling to sin.

I got a letter from someone one time who had been listening to some of my tapes. This person said, "You ruined my fun." I replied, "Praise the Lord!" People say one of the big reasons they hesitate to really get serious with God, to get into a devotional life and make this their top priority, is because they are afraid that God is going to change them. They're afraid that God will mess up their lifestyle and maim them and cripple them. But we forget that God knows what He's doing and we can trust Him. This is what this strange analogy is all about: Plucking out the eye or cutting off the foot is God's work. But remember, He is a gentle surgeon, and we can trust Him.

---

1. Francis D. Nichol, ed., *Seventh-day Adventist Bible Commentary* (Hagerstown, Maryland: Review and Herald, 1956), 5:337.

2. Ibid.

3. Ibid., quoting Ellen G. White, *The Desire of Ages* (Nampa, Idaho: Pacific Press®, 1940), p. 123.

4. Ellen G. White, *Thoughts From the Mount of Blessing* (Nampa, Idaho: Pacific Press®, 1956), 61.

5. Ellen G. White, *Steps to Christ* (Hagerstown, Maryland: Review and Herald, 1956), 47.

6. Ibid., 48.

7. Ellen G. White, *Christ's Object Lessons* (Nampa, Idaho: Pacific Press®, 1952), 159.

Chapter 3

Eight Unclean Devils

Jesus told an interesting parable that's found in Matthew 12:43-45. It is a parable of eight devils, or eight unclean spirits. He said:

> When an evil spirit [or "unclean spirit," KJV] comes out of a man, it goes through arid places seeking rest and does not find it. Then it says, "I will return to the house I left." When it arrives, it finds the house unoccupied, swept clean and put in order. Then it goes and takes with it seven other spirits more wicked than itself, and they go in and live there. And the final condition of that man is worse than the first. That is how it will be with this wicked generation.

At first glance it doesn't look like there is much love in this parable, only warning. But I'd like to help us see that Jesus warned us because He loved us, and that even His scathing rebukes were given with tears in His voice. Let's try and see a loving heart in this hard-hitting parable.

Notice that we can understand this parable as speaking of a whole generation of people or a whole race of people who have disappointed God. We can also approach it as applying to a denomination or organized religion in general or to a specific local church. It may also speak to our family or to ourselves as individuals. So, let's sit up and give it a good look.

First of all we notice that, according to the King James Version, this is an *unclean* spirit. I don't know how many clean devils there are out there, but this was an unclean one. It's interesting to note that the King James Version uses the term "an unclean devil" in another story. It says, "In the synagogue there was a man, which had a spirit of an unclean devil, and cried out with a loud voice" (Luke 4:33).

It was an unclean devil, there in Capernaum, who came in and disrupted the service through this devil-possessed man. Well, I would like to see a clean devil. I think that I would prefer clean to unclean. Nonetheless, perhaps there are some clean devils whose major purpose in life is to get people to clean up their act by the force of will. Clean up their act to preserve their reputation. Clean up their act to try and earn their way to heaven. It could be that there's a whole quorum of clean devils out there who have that as their mission. They are not the ones involved in getting people to lie in their own vomit in the gutter. They are the ones who appeal to cleanness *apart from God,* which might make them just as devilish as the devils who get people in the gutter. Because you can go to hell in a respectable way; you don't always have to go in the gutter.

The parable says that the unclean spirit goes out of a man. Right here we run into a major question: Does he go out of this person by choice, by command, or under duress? If you check the commentaries, you'll discover that there are opposite viewpoints. My first impression from reading it simply from Scripture was that the devil never leaves voluntarily. This has to be talking about the genuine, converted life and the devil leaving under pressure from a mightier power, like the Holy Spirit. And I also remembered what I had discovered earlier concerning our walk with God—that we must be dependent upon God at every moment or the enemy will get us. So, how could we here have the devil leaving on his own?

However, there is no conflict indicated in this parable. There is no apparent struggle, no repentance, no brokenness of spirit, like the sinners who come to Christ weeping and cognizant of their filthy rags. Perhaps this parable is talking about a type of thing in which the unclean spirit is happy to leave by his own choice. Perhaps he has bigger ends to accomplish by leaving on his own. Maybe he wants to encourage the impression that a person can live a clean life without the indwelling of God for a time. But he is bound to come back—which is what Jesus was saying. In the same chapter, Jesus said, "If Satan drives out Satan, he is divided against himself. How then can his kingdom stand?" (verse 26). So, Jesus is here indicating that Satan isn't going to cast out Satan. But Satan might leave by his own choice for his own reasons.

I would like to propose that it is possible for Satan to *appear* to cast out Satan. And this gets really tricky, because when it appears that Satan has cast out Satan, we misunderstand it as being a genuine manifestation of the power of God. This is where Satan is very subtle. Although it is still true that Satan will never cast out Satan, yet perhaps he will go out by his own choice for a time and for a reason.

This parable could also be describing us as we gather together in a church or a group to pray and ask for the Holy Spirit's presence, which makes the evil spirits nervous and edgy and might even cause them to leave for a time, until "tomorrow." It could be that we experience this presence that is mighty in power, and we leave the sanctuary with a heart that has been vacated by the enemy only to find ourselves victims of the seven other devils as the week progresses. Whatever the case, it is a solemn consideration. Jesus apparently told this parable so we could see the difference between conviction and conversion.

The Holy Spirit is involved in some major works in our lives: First of all, He *convicts* the world of sin (see John 16:8). But that's not enough. *Everybody* is convicted of sin. So, second, He *converts* the sinner. Only those who kneel at the foot of the cross and accept the friendly invitation of the Holy Spirit are converted, or born again (see John 3:3-8). Possibly, then, this parable speaks of the people who are convicted of sin and then begin trying to expel sin from their own lives, only to be faced with a vacuum. Perhaps it is talking about people who have a changed life but not a changed heart. It is possible to have a changed life for a number of reasons—particularly if you are among the strong-willed—without having a changed heart. It is talking about a person who is reformed but not renewed or revived, a person who is a victim of religiousness but not spirituality. In any case, whatever they experience in terms of the absence of the unclean spirits, apparently, is going to be followed by an impasse.

NO REST FOR THE SPIRIT

Next in the story, the unclean spirit goes out seeking rest in dry places and finds none. What are the dry places? The main clue that I picked up was in the prophecy in Revelation 17:15, where people, multitudes, tongues, and kindreds are represented by water. So, a desolate, dry place would mean the absence of people.

Here we have the evil spirit going out looking for rest, and evil spirits don't find rest in dry places. In fact, evil spirits don't find rest at all. They are extremely restless, as you may know. Can you imagine what the evil spirits are going to feel like during the millennium, when there are no people? All the wicked are dead on the earth, and all the righteous are in heaven. The earth is vacated. There will be plenty of dry places. And Satan and his angels are here in discord with each other. If that were me, I think I would commit suicide during the first week. But they can't even do that.

Evil spirits are always restless. And they try to find meaning in their lives and try to overcome their restlessness by feverish activity and by causing people pain and trouble and heartache and sorrow. Sometimes we experience the same kind of restlessness. We feel the touch of the Holy Spirit, in terms of our own convictions and things of eternal life, and we get the fidgets. We get restless. So we make up for it by busyness, by being always on the go or by always having something going so we don't have to think. The enemy apparently is very familiar with this.

So, the unclean spirit seeks rest and finds none. Then he says, "I will return to the house I left." And here is another clue that he might have left voluntarily: "I will return to the house *I* left." He didn't move out. He only took a trip to Arizona, to the dry places, and he intends to come back—back to "*my* house." So he comes back. And the first thing we notice is that there is no opposition; there is no resistance. There is no one there to put up a fuss at his return. In fact, he knocks at the door and there is no answer. There should have been. There should be. Like the little girl who said, "When the devil comes and knocks at my heart's door, I ask Jesus to go to the door. He opens the door, and the devil says, 'Pardon me, I think I got the wrong address.' " Or, as someone else said, "The devil knocks on the door. Jesus goes to the door and says,

'Venden doesn't live here anymore. He's moved out.' " Yes. Instead, however, in this parable, there was nothing, no answer. So, he pushes the door open. No resistance. He hollers, "Anyone home?" And all he hears is an echo. Empty. Swept and garnished.

There is something about an empty house that is sort of sad. During my last year of working as a full-time minister before I retired, I had to travel back and forth between Arkansas, where my wife was living, and Southern California, where I was still pastoring. I would return from Arkansas to an empty house. It was kind of quiet. An empty house, however it may be decorated, is still desolate. There are ghostly shadows at the windows, and the floors creak. Every footfall echoes ominously, and in the hollow distance there is a slamming of the door. Moreover, an empty house never remains empty. Rodents claim the forsaken rooms, rats run through the closets, and spiders spin their webs. I hate it when I feel those webs all around my neck.

In the same way, the house of life, when left empty, invites undesirable tenants. Former evil habits prey upon it. Finally, overcome with disappointment over our failures to reform, we deliver the house to abandonment and despair. An empty house—that's what the unclean spirit comes back to. Jesus said, "It finds the house unoccupied, swept clean, and put in order." Perhaps he goes to the door to check the doorposts to see if there is any blood there, because if there is blood, as in the Passover of old, then he knows that his day is done. But there is no blood there. The house is swept and garnished.

What does sweeping mean? We sweep what is loose. We sweep up the loose dust and dirt and things. We get our moral brooms and try to sweep our sins away—the loose sins from our loose living. Our sweeping might even appear to work for a while. Perhaps we don't drink or smoke or gamble anymore, but what about the other sins, such as pride, envy, rudeness, and self-seeking? Sweeping away our moral dust is not enough.

The King James Version says the house was "swept and garnished." What is that? What is "garnished"? People who are empty on the inside will often fall for religious trimmings and will garnish the emptiness with pictures: maybe pictures of Jesus, or a crucifix, or beautiful flowers, or ornaments of other people's experiences, people we like to read about—anything that will cover up their emptiness. Perhaps the garnishment takes the form of doing service for the church or giving to the poor and needy or long prayers. Or it can be the garnishment of zeal and excitement, or the garnishment of emotion—going to church each week to get our emotions pumped up. The garnishments can come in all flavors and forms. Thus, the enemy finds the house swept and garnished, because the less you have on the inside, the more you have to put on the outside.

It is a mystery to some of us why we can lower the standards we used to hold and give people an opportunity to advertise in their adornment on the outside how empty they are on the inside. The fact remains that the less you have inside, the more you have to garnish the outside. Why do we want to advertise that? But we do. And we do it in terms of the spiritual life and the heart that is void of the Holy Spirit.

Well, this unclean spirit thinks that what he's found is too good for one spirit. So, he goes out and gets seven other spirits to join him. And they come back. It says that he gets seven spirits more wicked than himself. You mean there are some spirits who are more wicked than others? Apparently so. Maybe this is in contrast with those "clean devils." Anyway, we're talking about the ultimate in wickedness in this case. Here we are reminded of Mary from Magdala, who was a victim of seven devils according to Scripture. We are also reminded of the homosexuals on the other side of the Sea of Galilee in the cemetery of the Gadarenes. You say, "Are homosexuals mentioned?" Apparently so. I didn't realize it until I read it in the book *The Desire of Ages*.[1] Matthew 8 says these two men who inhabited the tombs were involved in the most despicable forms of degradation. It also says that they were inhabited by legions—*legions*—of evil spirits. Not just one, or seven, but legions.

The exciting thing is that Jesus can control legions of evil spirits with a word. It is important that in any discussion we don't dwell totally on the evil spirits. We need to magnify the name of Jesus and be thankful that in His presence we have nothing to fear. Because evil spirits tremble in His presence.

WORSE OFF THAN BEFORE

The parable says that these evil spirits enter in and dwell in the empty house. This is the same language that the Bible uses in appealing to us to invite Christ to dwell in our hearts by faith. This is the bottom line of the Christian life—instead of the enemy dwelling within, Jesus dwelling within, so that we can understand with all the saints what is the height and breadth and length of the love of God. In this case, however, the devils enter and dwell there. And Jesus said the last state of that man is worse than the first.

So, if we're just approaching this parable from a human viewpoint, we would conclude that the man would have been better off if the unclean spirit had never left or had never been cast out, because afterwards he was indwelt by eight evil spirits. It might be better for a church or congregation to never hear the message of righteousness by faith, because if the congregation doesn't do anything about it, the last state of that church might be worse than the first. It might be better if a denomination never hears the message of the true gospel, because it lays a heavy responsibility on the organized church, and unless the message is heeded, the last state of that church might be worse than the first. It might be better for a family or an individual to never hear the gospel, humanly speaking, because it makes families and individuals have the fidgets. The last state of anyone who hears the gospel will be worse than before they got the message unless they deal with it properly. And we're not talking about a few short years here. We're talking about eternity. Eternal life is at stake. Unless I get the message of this story and find the secret of eternal life, it would have been better if I had never been born.

The last state of the person who has once had a genuine faith and walked away from it is worse than the first and is usually a sample of the greatest degradation and debauchery. I have accumulated some case histories of this over my forty years of trying to be a pastor. There are some sad wrecks in the sands of life—people who got the message and walked away from it and did nothing about it; people who enjoyed the services on Sabbath and did nothing about them during the week, who listened to the Good News and walked away from the life of faith. This can happen to congregations. It is a solemn, solemn thought. Probably the greatest case history of one who walked away from closeness to God is Satan himself—Lucifer, the son of the morning. And who could equal the debauchery and degeneration that has taken place in his life? Another example is Judas, one of Jesus' closest followers, who ended up walking away and letting the unclean spirits come back in and lead him to betray his own Creator. It would have been better for Judas if he had never been born.

Now, we come to one of the main thrusts of this story. It's found in the context of the parable. We notice that Jesus was trying to indicate that there is another way to get the devil out, whether casting him out or letting him go out on his own choice. It is something that we consider today when dealing with medicine, child training, or psychology. Ill health must be driven out by the incoming of nature's own vitality. I understand that most of us, if not all of us, are subject to cancer "germs" all the time. But generally, those cancer germs don't multiply until our vitality is down. If ill health is not conquered by nature's own vitality, its expulsion is not permanent and a relapse is to be feared. Medicine now concerns itself not only with the process of cure, but with the establishment and maintenance of health.

Not too long ago I met a doctor who was old enough to retire, but who told me that he was just beginning his practice.

"What do you mean?" I asked in surprise.

He said, "I've been ripping people off for forty years."

"You have?"

"Yes, by giving them what they wanted—prescriptions for dealing with their symptoms," he explained. "But now I'm into preventive medicine, and I can hardly wait to get to the office."

Similarly, modern methods of child training recommend that parents should stop the "don't do that" kind of discipline and substitute in place of the wrong activity, a new and proper interest. So, instead of telling my child, "Don't do that on Sabbath," I say, "Let's do this in place of that."

Recent psychology reiterates the same truth. What is to be done with a dark memory or a cherished grudge? It must be driven out. The demon must be exorcised. To bury a dark memory, to let it remain as an evil tenant in my subconscious is to spread its fullness. The expulsion of the presence is not enough. That conquest is merely preliminary. The obsession, bitterness, or remorse must then be reassociated, they say. It must be absorbed in a legitimate and more passionate purpose. It must be linked with a new, sound attitude of life. The house must be occupied by its rightful tenant.

Though many voices proclaim this truth, however, religion has been slow to hear and heed. We are so ready to banish the demons, but we are so loath to welcome Jesus. Yet when He comes to rule, the demons flee of themselves—which means, in short, that we never stamp out evil, Jesus crowds it out when He enters. This is why the daily relationship with God is so significant. Jesus crowds evil out when He enters. And when the enemy comes back from seeking rest and finding none, he finds the house inhabited, and inhabited well. There is no room for him. He has to go on his way. When Jesus comes in, the devil stays out.

I read a couple one-liners in *The Desire of Ages* that I think are very significant: "Whenever men reject the Savior's invitation, they are yielding themselves to Satan."[2]

"Oh," I say, "I'm not under the control of demons! I live a good moral life."

That's not the issue. If I don't have time for Jesus day by day, I'm allowing Satan to control my direction, and he's sending me down. Whether I know it or not, I'm going down. And sooner or later I will discover that he is not only controlling my direction, but he is controlling *me*.

The other one-liner pictures the brighter side, the more beautiful one—this good news: "Those who will consent to enter into covenant relation with the God of heaven are not left to the power of Satan or to the infirmity of their own nature."[3] What a difference! Being controlled by God or being controlled by the enemy.

I read the prayer Spurgeon prayed following a sermon he preached about this parable. It was probably the most significant part of his attempt to address the parable. I've read a lot of Spurgeon, and I have the impression that the Holy Spirit must have taken hold of him in a special way at the moment he prayed. His prayer has the old English sound to it, but see if you can't pick up its impact:

> My Lord Jesus, if thou art passing by, traveling in the greatness of thy strength, come and show thy vaunted powers. Turn aside, thou heavenly Samson, and win the lion in the vineyard. If thou hast dipped thy robes in the blood of thy cross, come dye them all again with the blood of my sins. If thou has trodden the winepress of Jehovah's wrath and crushed thy enemies, here is another of the accursed crew, come and drag him out and crush him. Here is an Agag in my heart, come and hew him in pieces. Here is a dragon in my spirit, break oh break his head and set me free from my old state of sin. Deliver me from my fierce enemy and unto thee be the praise for ever and ever. Amen.

As I read that, I thought about two people: Nicodemus and Joseph of Arimathea. They didn't identify with Jesus until the very end. They were victims of a society and a generation that had it all wrong. They waited and waited. But God doesn't give up. At the end they came out and identified strongly with the early church. They provided a decent burial for the Lord Jesus and encouraged His followers.

You and I can be among those, who, like Joseph and Nicodemus, step forward and accept the invitation of Jesus to make sure that, as we approach the end of time, our hearts are inhabited by the God above, by the Holy Spirit, and by Jesus, who loves us.

---

1. See Ellen G. White, *The Desire of Ages* (Nampa, Idaho: Pacific Press®, 1940), 339, 341.
2. Ibid., 341.
3. Ibid., 258, 259.

Chapter 4

The Sower, the Seed, and the Soil

Have you ever planted a garden? Probably most of us can remember working in the soil, planting those radish seeds with a little help from Mom or Dad. (Why was it always radishes?) We would go to bed and then rush out first thing in the morning to see how the radishes were coming, right? Remember what came up first? It wasn't radishes—it was the weeds!

I know what I did as soon as the first little radish sprouts appeared—and perhaps I wasn't the only person ever to do such a thing. I pulled them up to see if there were any radishes. I can remember pulling one a day to see how they were coming along—and that didn't help things a bit. If they didn't come up after a few days, I would go and dig for them, to see where they were. I've even done that with grass seed!

There's a lot to be learned out there in the garden. Jesus used parables about the garden on more than one occasion. In fact, it seemed to be one of His favorite sources of illustrations about the kingdom of heaven.

Let's look at one of His major parables:

> While a large crowd was gathering and people were coming to Jesus from town after town, he told this parable: "A farmer went out to sow his seed. As he was scattering the seed, some fell along the path; it was trampled on, and the birds of the air ate it up. Some fell on rock, and when it came up, the plants withered because they had no moisture. Other seed fell among thorns, which grew up with it and choked the plants. Still other seed fell on good soil. It came up and yielded a crop, a hundred times more than was sown."
>
> When he said this, he called out, "He who has ears to hear, let him hear."
>
> His disciples asked him what this parable meant (Luke 8:4-9).

When Jesus says, "He who has ears to hear, let him hear," then the message must be rather important. So let's try to hear what He was saying in this parable about the sower, the seed, and the soil.

THE SYMBOLS

The Farmer. Whom does the farmer represent? The farmer is Jesus—He was referring to Himself. He came from the city that has jasper walls and twelve foundations to an unfriendly country.

In the days of Christ, farmers didn't live out on the farm. They were village farmers. It wasn't safe to stay out in the country. The cities had walls for protection. You can go to parts of the world today where the remains of the cities of those days still stand. They had walls to keep people safe from robbers and thieves and murderers. The unfortunate man who was beaten up by the thieves on the Jericho Road and was helped by the good Samaritan was an example of what things were like in the days of Jesus. Farmers lived in the city behind safe walls and went out into the countryside in the daytime to sow their seed.

Jesus left a friendly city, a heavenly city, where He was adored by angels and the entire created universe worshiped before Him. He came to an unfriendly country, outside the walls of safety—to a place of thieves and robbers and murderers. He took all the risks necessary to plant the seed. This is the kind of person the farmer was.

Do you like to think of Jesus as a farmer? It's not Farmer Brown or Farmer Jones; it's Farmer Jesus. How does that sound? It's not irreverent to call Him Farmer Jesus, for in His life here on this earth, He put His stamp of approval on hard physical work. He's the One who worked for eighteen years in the carpenter shop in Nazareth, planing wood and sawing boards.

I'm glad that Jesus didn't live in a palace, aren't you? I'm glad that Jesus was a poor person who knew the meaning of hard work. By being this kind of person He could reach everybody. And so He went forth to sow.

The Seed. What is the seed? Jesus explains the parable, so you know—if you've read the rest of Luke 8—that the seed is the Word of God. Nothing more, nothing less. The Word of God has power to produce life and growth and fruit from the soul.

It still can today. Sometimes we try to meet people with philosophy and psychology and all kinds of things. Sometimes we think our boys and girls need entertainment or gimmicks to keep their attention. We need to remember the power that is in the Word of God, which "liveth and abideth forever." When we join Jesus in sowing the seed of the gospel, we need to remember that it is the Word of God that is the seed. That's where it's at.

The Soil. But what about the soil? Jesus mentioned four kinds of soil. It sounds almost like predestination, doesn't it? Were you born as the hard-packed wayside or as rocky soil or as thorny soil? Or were you born with good soil? Do you think you can identify which kind of soil is in your own heart? What if you discover that the soil in your heart is no good? Is there anything you can do about it? Keep these questions in mind as we think about the four kinds of soil Jesus talked about in this parable.

The Path. The path—or "wayside," as the King James Version has it—is ground that is packed down and hard from being tramped on. If it isn't actually the path, it's at least right next to it. It's the ground alongside the road that is almost as hard as the road itself. It's where the brown paper bags lie, and the broken bottles, and the M&M wrappers. It is filled with debris. It's not an attractive place, and certainly not a good place to sow seed.

It could represent the kind of people who have a hard-beaten path from their house to the church, but who have allowed the debris of cherished sin and habit and neglect to fill up their life. The wayside ground is not subject to change—in fact, it is resistant to change. The wayside hearers believe that whatever was good enough for Father and Mother is good enough for them. Their religion is conventional and consists of going through the forms. If there's a crack in the clutter where the seed can fall and spring up, then the birds come along and get it—and there are plenty of hungry birds in the kingdom of this world.

So the seed that falls onto the wayside ground doesn't stand much of a chance. If we are able to squeeze Jesus into the cracks, that's about all He can expect. There is no hope for a harvest or for fruit to His glory. The prospects aren't good for the heart with the wayside soil.

Rocky Soil. Let's consider the second type of soil, the rocky soil. You'd think that the seed that falls there doesn't have much of a chance either. But even among rocks there usually is a bit of dust, and it's amazing what can spring up after a rain—tiny green shoots on what looks like bare rock. These might last for half a day, or maybe for a day and a half. But they don't last long, because there isn't enough soil for them to take root. The sun scorches them, or the next rain washes them away, and they are gone.

Rocky soil could represent the kind of religious experience that is here today and gone tomorrow—the kind of person who can go through a revival and an apostasy all the same week. This could represent the emotional religion, dependent upon the right singing, the right nostalgia, the right tear-jerking stories. But soon after the emotional high is over, things are right back where they started.

This soil represents the people who respond only with their emotions. Such an experience is neither deep nor lasting—it is just the impulse of the moment, just the reaction for the day. It is a sort of rock-and-roll religion that works the nervous system but doesn't change the heart. There may be a seeming conversion under the thrill of the moment. But as soon as the stimulus is removed, the spiritual life dies out—sometimes overnight. Prospects aren't good for the heart with the rocky soil.

Thorny Ground. Some seed fell on thorny ground. We find thorns and weeds are everywhere, don't we? They don't require cultivation. They can spring up spontaneously. When our family lived in Nebraska a few years ago, we had a seven-acre piece of ground that was covered with those purple thistles. The weeds seemed to multiply a thousand times over every spring and summer—and they didn't require any work, either. If we'd wanted to raise purple thistles, we could have just lain in the hammock and let it happen!

Well, some seed fell among the thorns, and even though the soil underneath might have been all right, there were too many thorns. Many of us, perhaps, identify with this soil. We might argue as to whether or not we are wayside or rocky soil, but there's no mistaking thorny ground. It's easy to see the thorns in our lives, the things that choke out the good seed.

What are some of these thorns? They could be the pleasures of the world—maybe even innocent pleasures, like playing tennis, for instance! Something that is good in itself becomes a thorn when it crowds out the good seed. Another kind of thorn weed would be life's cares, perplexities, and sorrows. There are plenty of these to demand our attention, no matter who we are. The problem of keeping body and soul together can take a lot of time and energy. The poor fear for want, and the rich for loss. Both can become preoccupied with the cares of this life.

Thorns can take the form of sorrow and heartache. These are the common lot of humanity, but some of us allow the devil to turn them into thorns—thorns that prevent us from seeing Jesus anymore. Then there are the faults of others. How many times have people stumbled over the faults of those around them? We've all experienced it to some degree. The faults of others can become thorns if we allow them to keep our attention from Jesus and the things of heaven. And our own faults and imperfections can accomplish the same thing.

What can one do about thorns—the weeds and thistles that prevent the growth of the gospel seed? There are a lot of thorns out there—and prospects don't look good for the heart with the thorny soil.

The Good Soil. What is the good soil? It is those who receive the seed with an honest and good heart. That sounds appealing, doesn't it? Do you have an honest heart, a good heart? How many hearts of that kind are there?

We often hear people pray for the "honest in heart." Have you ever heard anyone pray for the Lord's blessing on the dishonest in heart? One day I actually heard someone say, "Lord, bless all the dishonest in heart!" Surely they need some prayers too.

One time at a camp meeting I heard the speaker get up and ask, "How many of you have been praying for Khrushchev?" Not a hand was raised. Then he said, "I've been praying for Khrushchev lately. He seems to be standing in the need of prayer. I think he'd make a wonderful preacher, don't you?"

What about the apostle Paul? Before his experience on the Damascus Road, he certainly didn't appear to be a good candidate for leadership in the early church. He is frequently depicted holding the coats of the men who were stoning Stephen. But that was just the beginning. From doing that he went on to become directly responsible for the death and imprisonment of many of the Christian believers. He tells us so.

But God could see into his heart, and He saw good soil there. One day He stepped in and stopped Saul in his tracks, and Saul became Paul, the mighty preacher and evangelist and author and missionary.

How can we judge what is in someone's heart? We don't know the roots, the background of those around us. Only God knows what makes an honest heart. Only He knows where the good soil is to be found—and some of the places that hold good soil surprise many of us.

What is good soil? Here are a few clues. It is soil that yields to the conviction of the Holy Spirit, admits its need, and maintains a continual, personal receiving of life from the heavenly Gardener. It is in this kind of soil that the perfect fruit of faith and meekness and love matures.

Is a person simply predestined to be good soil? Or wayside soil? Or rocky soil? Or thorny soil? And if one isn't predestined to be a particular kind of soil, how does one become good soil?

Jesus never taught predestination. The Bible doesn't teach it. This parable is saying that every heart contains all four kinds of soil.

EVERY KIND OF SOIL

Haven't you noticed that your heart contains some of each kind of soil? We all know what it's like to be wayside soil on some things, if not on all things. If someone gets up and talks against a sin that I disapprove, I'm good soil. My folks, for instance, raised me with certain inhibitions. Some things do not appeal to me simply because of my tastes and inclinations and personality. So when I hear those things condemned, I'm good soil. But if someone gets up and talks against one of my besetting sins, all of a sudden I'm wayside soil.

So our hearts can have wayside soil or rocky soil or thorny soil on one thing and good soil on something else. We have all experienced it and find that even when it comes to the gospel itself and relating to the call of Jesus to the human heart, we give mixed responses. But there is good soil in every heart. And the great Farmer, the Sower of the seed, Jesus Himself, is anxious to reach that good soil with the seed of the gospel. He will try every means possible to reach the good soil in your heart and sow the seed of His Word, that it may produce a harvest to His glory.

I wish I didn't have thorny soil. I don't like the hardness I sometimes feel in my heart. Sometimes I find it hard to change some of my ideas. But can I do anything about it? Have you ever tried to get the weeds out of your soul soil? What can I do to help the Gardener rid my life of thorns and stones and hard-packed earth? Here's a parable that may help you think this through.

WHAT CAN THE SOIL DO?

Once there was a plot of ground that wanted to be a garden. The Farmer purchased this plot at great expense. He then obtained some seed of excellent quality and came to the plot of ground and sowed the seed.

Well, the plot of ground rejoiced. It had always wanted to be a garden. And it began immediately to try to do its part toward becoming a garden of beauty and fruitfulness. It began to look at itself, and it discovered to its dismay that it was covered with unsightly weeds—thorns and thistles and briers and brambles. The plot was concerned and ashamed. Before the coming of the Farmer, it hadn't paid much attention to such things, so the weeds had made terrible inroads. Their roots were deeply entrenched in the soil.

"How can I receive any benefit from the seed while all these weeds are growing unchecked?" wondered the plot of ground. "Everyone knows that a garden must be weeded in order for the seed to grow."

So it began immediate efforts to remove the weeds. It wanted to cooperate with the Farmer so that as soon as possible it would no longer be just an ugly weed patch, but would instead be a lovely garden.

The plot of ground struggled and fretted. It sincerely wanted to get rid of its weeds, but the problem was figuring out how. All the instructions about weed pulling seemed to be vague and contradictory. The plot of ground heard from one source that if it would get rid of the leaves and stems, the Farmer would then be willing to pull out the roots. But it discovered it was too weak to get rid of the leaves and stems.

It was told that if a plot of ground did its part, then the Farmer would do His part. But the plot of ground seemed unable to do any part of the weed pulling for itself. It was often told to try hard to overcome the weeds, but it didn't know how to do that either. So, when the weeds were still apparent week after week, those around the plot of ground and even the plot of ground itself began to wonder if it were really sincere in wanting to get rid of the weeds.

Someone suggested to the plot of ground that the job would be easier if it wouldn't try to remove all the weeds from the garden at once but would concentrate on removing just one weed at a time. But the plot of ground found itself unable to remove even one weed.

At times the plot of ground almost gave up in discouragement at the lack of progress made, but then it would once again picture the garden it longed to become, and it would again put forth earnest efforts to try to get rid of the weeds. But all of the efforts of the plot of ground to rid itself of the thorns and briers ended in nothing.

One day the plot of ground was forced to admit that it would never become a beautiful garden on its own. That very day the Farmer came to the plot of ground with some terrific news. (The Farmer had come often before, but the plot of ground had been so busy struggling with the weeds that it hadn't taken time to listen.) The Farmer told the plot of ground something that was almost impossible to believe. It seemed to go contrary to everything the plot of ground had ever heard about gardening. Here is what the Farmer said: "It is not the responsibility of the garden to get rid of the weeds. That is the work of the Gardner."

Well, you can see right away why the plot of ground had trouble with the Farmer's announcement. But unless the plot of ground accepted the Farmer's offer, it must give up all hope of becoming a beautiful garden. So the plot of ground surrendered to the Farmer and allowed Him to pull the weeds. And the first thing you know, the weeds were being removed—and not just the leaves and stems— the entire plants were being uprooted and taken far from the plot of ground. Then, in their place, the good seeds that had been sown in the garden began to grow and develop.

As time passed, the plot of ground, which was now a beautiful garden, continued to allow the Farmer to do His work. And the garden continued to do its work—it continued to accept the seed that the Farmer sowed, drank deeply of the water the Farmer showered on it, and basked in the sunshine that the Farmer provided. The plants in the garden grew and grew and brought forth fruit— some an hundredfold, some sixty, and some thirty.

Chapter 5

The Wheat and the Weeds

I went into a feed-and-seed store in Rogers, Arkansas, one day to ask for some help. The clerk said, "Can I hep you?"

I said, "Yeah. Y'all can sell me some fescue. I want to buy some fescue to plant the lawn with."

I didn't ask for any of those purple thistles. I didn't ask for any cockle weeds or Bermuda grass. I didn't even ask for St. Augustine grass, which some of us have struggled with for years in Southern California. I wanted pure, all-pro fescue.

They didn't even have purple thistle at the store. They didn't have cockle or darnel. They had pure fescue. But somewhere along the line someone got those purple thistles going, and the cockle weeds, and the Bermuda grass, and the St. Augustine grass. And I said to myself, "An enemy has done this."

This experience reminds me of one of the great stories Jesus told, the story about the weeds in the field. In this story He addresses the question of why a good God lets evil continue—a question that has plagued people for a long time. Now, I suppose, we could go directly to the short-answer version that many are familiar with, the one found in Philippians 2:10. There the Bible predicts that the day is coming when every knee is going to bow and every tongue is going to confess that Jesus Christ is Lord and that God is good. They are not doing that now. Many people take the name of Jesus on their lips only in cursing. But soon the day will come when every knee will bow. Apparently this is one of the reasons why God allows evil to run its course so that it will never come up the second time. The story of the wheat and the weeds reveals this:

> Jesus told them another parable: "The kingdom of heaven is like a man who sowed good seed in his field. But while everyone was sleeping, his enemy came and sowed weeds among the wheat, and went away. When the wheat sprouted and formed heads, then the weeds also appeared.
>
> The owner's servants came to him and said, "Sir, didn't you sow good seed in your field? Where then did the weeds come from?"
>
> "An enemy did this," he replied.
>
> The servants asked him, "Do you want us to go and pull them up?"
>
> "No," he answered, "because while you are pulling the weeds, you may root up the wheat with them. Let both grow together until the harvest. At that time I will tell the harvesters: First collect the weeds and tie them in bundles to be burned; then gather the wheat and bring it into my barn" (Matthew 13:24-30).

No doubt Jesus told stories because He likes children and children like stories. But He told stories for a couple other reasons too.

He told them to reveal truth to those who were listening and to conceal truth from those who didn't want to hear anyway.

Matthew 13 contains several parables Jesus told to the crowd. The disciples knew that they could get an explanation from Him later. So the story picks up again in verse 36, after the crowd had been dismissed:

> Then he left the crowd and went into the house. His disciples came to him and said, "Explain to us the parable of the weeds in the field."
>
> He answered, "The one who sowed the good seed is the Son of Man. The field is the world, and the good seed stands for the sons of the kingdom. The weeds are the sons of the evil one, and the enemy who sows them is the devil. The harvest is the end of the age, and the harvesters are angels.
>
> "As the weeds are pulled up and burned in the fire, so it will be at the end of the age. The Son of Man will send out his angels, and they will weed out of his kingdom everything that causes sin and all who do evil. They will throw them into the fiery furnace, where there will be weeping and gnashing of teeth. Then the righteous will shine like the sun in the kingdom of their Father. He who has ears, let him hear" (Matthew 13:36-43).

What is Jesus trying to tell us here? Let's look at this from three perspectives: the first one, the field as the world; the second, the field as the church; and the third, the field as your heart and mine.

THE FIELD IS THE WORLD

First, the field as the world in which an enemy has been at work and has accomplished his ends successfully. Who is going to argue that an enemy has or has not been at work in our world? Who can explain sin and its beginning in heaven, with Lucifer, the Son of the Morning, who fell? How can we explain weeds coming up with no one to start them? It's a mystery. But it happened. Then the enemy became the person with forty names, called by all different kinds of names in the Bible, who has wreaked havoc and destruction ever since.

There are two great powers in the universe: good and evil. You don't have to go to your Bible to hear about it. You can go to drama and theater and entertainment. *Star Wars,* the popular movie series, depicts the conflict between the two powers, good and evil. It's everywhere: the good guys and the bad guys, the white hats and the black hats. An enemy has done this—heartache and tears, pain and sorrow, tombstones and monuments to broken hearts and funeral trains and hospitals; the troubles and bumps and bruises of planet Earth. Jesus said, "An enemy has done this."

We know who he is. He's been a prisoner of God ever since his fall.

A prisoner of God?

Yes. Because if the wages of sin is death, the devil should have been dead a long time ago, shouldn't he? He should have died of coronary aneurysms and cancer and thromboses and hardening of the arteries and nervous prostrations and whatever! He should have been dead a long time ago. But he goes on and on. If I were the devil, I think I would commit suicide. But he can't even do that. And he's miserable.

How do I know he's miserable? Because I read the advice columnists. You don't have to go to your Bible to find out that the devil is miserable. People whose lives are focused on themselves are miserable. And the one who wants to be happy has to become a dues-paying member of society. The people who are the happiest are the ones whose lives are directed outwards, toward others. And if the devil is as mean and icky as we say he is, and he is the number one sinner and the author of it all, then we know he's miserable. But he's trapped. He keeps on going. Life continues. He's a prisoner of God, as God in His wisdom allows the whole problem of evil to work itself out to its final end and waits for all the data to roll in and all the water to go under the bridge.

We've seen the wheat and the weeds in terms of technology. Some say that people who lived back before the Flood might have had some kind of advanced technology. But look at us in the past hundred years. Grandpa and Grandma, if they could be here, would be astonished at the growth in science and invention. We have been able to tap unheard of resources, and the energy available to us is awesome. But what have we done with it? We've fought big world wars and developed the ability to destroy ourselves. That which should have been wheat and good has left us in fear. Statesmen and scientists run scared because we have a problem. The wheat and the weeds grow together, and the weeds have caused panic in the hearts of many as we wonder what is going to happen next.

Someone asked Einstein, "What kind of weapons are we going to use in World War III?"

He said, "I can't tell you. But I'll tell you what kind we'll use in World War IV. Rocks." That's all that will be left, rocks.

So, the wheat and the weeds grow together in a world gone wrong. The righteous and the wicked live together until the end. That's the way it is in the story. And not until then, according to Malachi 3, will we be able to discern, really discern, between the righteous and the wicked.

In this story, the servants come along and ask, "Lord, shall we pull out the weeds?"

He says, "No. Leave them alone. Let them grow together until the harvest."

Have you ever wished that you could pull out the weeds? Shall we deal with it, or shall we follow what Jesus said and wait?

Perhaps we can notice three major reasons why we can't deal with the weeds at this time. First, evil is bigger than we are. If we could solve the problem of evil with social programs and marches on Washington, then we could soon be done with it. But social programs and marches on Washington don't deal with the human heart. Waving placards and shouting from the housetops about equality and race and cultures and genders don't change the hearts of people.

Second, we have weeds within our own hearts. We all struggle with the weeds. We are not all pure wheat. Are you? On the other hand, have you ever sat down and said, "Look, here is a total weed." I'm not talking about the neighbors' kids. I'm talking about a person who is totally all weeds. No, even in the worst of us there is some evidence of wheat. So, we find ourselves victims of the combination of wheat and weeds. And those of us who are desperate to go out and take care of all the weeds out there fall victims to the old adage, "It takes a thief to know a thief." We learned during our high school years that those who had a real burden—one string on their violin—and were going to take care of this or that evil were in reality advertising their own problem, because that was all they could think about.

A counselor says to the client, "Tell me what these drawings remind you of." Then the counselor draws a square and shows it to the client, and the client says, "Sex!"

The counselor draws a circle, "What does this remind you of?"

"Sex."

Then a triangle, "What does this remind you of?"

"Sex."

The counselor says, "You've got a problem."

And the client replies, "I've got a problem? You're the one who drew all these dirty pictures!"

This illustrates something that people have often discussed and pondered—that we become preoccupied with the evil in our own heart and then want to stamp it out in others. But it takes a thief to know a thief, and we are incapable of either perceiving evil or stamping it out, for we ourselves are victims of the same problem.

The third reason we can't deal with the weeds now is that Jesus' primary mission at this time is not to destroy the weeds but to harvest the wheat. He made it clear to His disciples over and over again that He did not come to destroy people. He came to save them. It makes no difference whether we are wheat or weeds. Jesus came to save us.

I ran into a snag on this parable because one of the commentaries said, "Weeds never become wheat." Maybe so, on the botanical level. But wait a minute! Jesus talked about the miracle of the new birth. People can be born again. So, could there be a miracle of the weed becoming wheat, or at least something that looks like a total weed becoming wheat? Jesus came not to destroy people's lives, including the Samaritans who were inhospitable to Him, the people whom the disciples wanted to punish with heaven's fire. He said, "You don't understand. I didn't come to destroy. I came to save." That is what He is interested in doing. If I find myself with both wheat and weeds in my heart, I can take courage. Jesus came to save people like me. Isn't that good news?

Now, let's take a look at this parable from the second perspective: The field is the church.

THE FIELD IS THE CHURCH

The church! Now we are getting a little closer to home. Have there been weeds in the church? Has there been an enemy at work? Has there been an enemy evangelist, if you please, who has been getting people to be converts to the church instead of to Christ? Does the church include people who are victims of dogma and points of doctrine, who do not know the regenerating power of the Holy Spirit? So, the church does have weeds. The church does experience the hindrance to the wheat—people who stir up strife, who want to be first, who love the praise of others. And the enemy who has done it knows that the greatest blow to the church comes from sabotage, enemy agents within—those who look like wheat, but are not wheat and only stir up trouble.

So, who are they? Who are the weeds? Why don't we have a dump-the-weeds campaign and get them all out?

We've got a problem. We don't know who they are. We have a hard time figuring out who they are.

Surveys have been taken on the campuses of Christian schools of many different faiths to try to find out how many of the students have actually been converted and are committed to Christ. These studies indicate that about 20 percent of the student body are committed Christians. And on any given year there are 20 percent who are hostile to God and faith and religion. They are on campus for other reasons. The remaining 60 percent are in between, willing to be led. And the tug-of-war goes on every school year.

When I heard about that, while pastoring on a Christian campus, I said, "Look, let's take care of the hostile 20 percent down at the admissions office. Let's throw them out before they even hit the campus." But when the school is in financial straits and all students have to do to get in is to be able to hear thunder and see lightning and have their checkbooks in their back pockets, the weeds get in.

But then the big surprises begin to come. We discover that often, with young people, the good guys with the white hats later trade places with the bad guys with the black hats. And it's hard to discern. Some of our great missionaries come from the former hostile ones. So, when we sit down and try to figure out who the weeds are, we go, "Ouch!" We misjudge again and again.

After watching the phenomena for a while, I was at an old-fashioned camp meeting one summer talking to the youth in the youth tent. All of a sudden, in the middle of the meeting, there was a great explosion. There must have been several packets of firecrackers going off at the edge of the tent. And because of these studies, I impulsively said, "Don't worry about them. They'll be great missionaries some day."

Yes, probably so. We have trouble trying to decide who's wheat and who's weeds.

I was reading about this parable in a little book called *Christ's Object Lessons,* and I found this interesting comment:

> Christ has plainly taught that those who persist in open sin must be separated from the church, but He has not committed to us the work of judging character and motive. He knows our nature too well to entrust this work to us. Should we try to uproot from the church those whom we suppose to be spurious Christians, we should be sure to make mistakes. Often we regard as hopeless subjects the very ones whom Christ is drawing to Himself.[1]

Not judgment and condemnation of others, but humility and distrust of self. That is the teaching of this parable. Don't try to pull out the weeds. That is God's responsibility. And only He knows when and how to do the least damage.

Jesus came from a heavenly country where trouble had arisen. How long did He wait before throwing Lucifer out? We're not told. But He worked and He pleaded and He hoped that the angels would listen. And then the day came when He moved in on the problem, and one-third of the wheat, now become weeds, left. Jesus came from a country where they knew the heartbreak and the pain of the wheat becoming weeds. So, we better trust the God who is all-wise when it comes to uprooting the weeds. There are souls in the Christian faith who are growing more slowly than others, and it would be too bad to strike down slow-growing souls because, in our judgment, they are not keeping up to speed.

And what about Jesus, who had a regard for the one who was to be His traitor? Explain that. Year after year He allowed a weed to grow with the wheat among the twelve disciples. Notice this modern version of the consultation agency in Jordan:

To Jesus, Son of Joseph
Woodcrafter Carpenter Shop
Nazareth 25922

Dear Sir,
Thank you for submitting the resumes of the twelve men you have picked for management positions in your new organization. All of them have now taken our battery of tests, and we have not only run the results through our computer but have also arranged personal interviews for each of them with our psychologist and vocational-aptitude consultants. The profiles of all tests are included, and you will want to study each of them carefully. As part of our service and for your guidance we make some general com-

ments, much as an auditor will include general statements. This is given as a result of staff consultation, and it comes without additional fee.

It is our staff's opinion that most of your nominees are lacking in background, education, and vocational aptitude for the type of enterprise you are undertaking. They do not have the team concept. We recommend that you continue your search for persons of experience with managerial ability and proven capacities.

Simon Peter is emotionally unstable and given to fits of temper. Andrew has absolutely no qualities of leadership. The two brothers, James and John, the sons of Zebedee, place personal interest above company loyalty. Thomas demonstrates a questioning attitude that would tend to undermine morale. We feel that it is our duty to tell you that Matthew has been blacklisted by the Greater Jerusalem Better Business Bureau. James the son of Alphaeus and Thaddeus definitely have radical leanings, and they both registered a high score on the manic-depressive scale.

One of the candidates, however, shows great potential. He is a man of ability and resourcefulness, meets people well, has a keen business mind, and has contacts in high places. He is highly motivated, ambitious, and responsible. We recommend Judas Iscariot as your controller and right-hand man. All of the other profiles are seriously questioned.

We wish you every success in your new venture.

Sincerely yours,
The Jordan Management Consultants

—Source Unknown

Yes, yes! That's the best we can do when it comes to differentiating between the weeds and the wheat. Could it be possible that

Jesus was following His own story in letting evil reach its natural outcome and by keeping close to Judas so He could counteract his influence? Shall we go so far as to say that Jesus kept Judas near so He could try to win him? We understand that Jesus almost got Judas the night He washed his feet in the upper room.

THE FIELD IS OUR HEART

To look at this parable from the third perspective is to look at the field of our heart. An enemy has been at work on our heredity and environment. Who is going to deny that we struggle with genes and chromosomes, with temperaments that have been handed down, with struggles that came all the way from Father Adam and Mother Eve? An enemy has been at work, and we have weeds in our own hearts. Have you recognized weeds in your own heart? I know I have. This is real. This is why fathers and mothers who bring their children for dedication fondly look over the cradle and the crib and hope against hope that the choices their little ones make will be for the kingdom of heaven.

But Hitler was once in the cradle. Nero, one of the world's great despots, was once in the cradle. No one changes from an innocent babe to a tyrant overnight. Yes, we struggle with the genes and the chromosomes and the environmental factors that continue to show that there is a sinister influence at work. The darkness startles us. We are concerned; we worry.

In our family planning, my wife and I decided that we would have two families. We would have two children and then we would wait ten years and have two more. That was the master plan. We had our first two children and waited ten years, but the equipment didn't quite work right the next time around. So, my wife began talking adoption. Adoption! Oh, we might get a criminal. And I began to brace my feet. "No way! What about those genes and chromosomes? You don't know . . ." But she continued to press. She didn't want to sit across the table from only me for all that time at the end of the line.

One day I said, "Well, let me know when the president of Harvard University and Miss America get together by mistake." She said, "You're not president of Harvard University." I said, "Neither are you Miss America." Well, it was nothing but pass the salt for a few days after that.

Then one day she tricked me. She brought a little bundle and placed it under the Christmas tree in a box, with a ribbon around it. The little one was from a foster home where they get these babies, preemies. It was a shock at first! But then it was sort of love at first sight, and before long we had the little one, a little daughter. She began to grow, and it was a real shocker to find out that perhaps she had less hereditary problems than the others did.

However, the hereditary factors go on. We know it, we see it, and we struggle with it in our own hearts. We get anxious, and sometimes we decide that we are going to root out the trouble ourselves. We forget that it is God who takes care of the weeds. It is God who handles the weeds in the world, in the church, and in our own hearts.

Sometimes we try to do it ourselves. But that doesn't work. Our lives get complicated and confused. We forget that God has the power. He has the wisdom. He has the perfect timing to reveal the real nature of the weed, or of the problem. We say that James and John were short-tempered. No, that wasn't the problem. We say that Peter was impetuous. No, that wasn't the problem. These are symptoms of the problem. What was the problem? It is an age-old one called self-sufficiency.

Jesus allowed the weed in Peter's heart to run its course and allowed him to fall. It took time. Peter had been converted, but he still continued with the kind of tricks for which the consulting managers at Jordan would have thrown him out of town. Jesus let time do its work in Peter's life until self-discovery came in shock treatment for him. He found himself clinging to the ground in the Garden of Gethsemane, where Jesus had spilled drops of blood for him, and he wished that he could die because he had denied Jesus. But he didn't die that night, even though Judas did. Instead, his life was changed because Jesus allowed him to discover the real problem in his life. And He may be allowing you and me to discover the problem in our lives.

Are you in shock because of the discovery of your life's real problem? Don't look at it as an enemy. It might be a friend. That discovery isn't easy. It wasn't easy for Peter as he clung to the ground wishing he could die because he had denied his Best Friend. But the gentle power from above allows us to discover the real problems in our own hearts. And throughout our journey, as we struggle with the bumps and bruises of life and as we struggle with the weeds in our own hearts, we have the promises of forgiveness, of mercy, and of patience.

The disciples had the assurance of forgiveness before they forsook Jesus that night. Peter had the assurance of forgiveness before he denied his Lord. Jesus told them that their names were written in heaven. He had said to them in the upper room before they left Him and before Peter cursed, "You are clean" (John 13:10). The atmosphere of forgiveness and love and patience goes on for the wheat as well as for the weeds.

Yes, God allows both the wheat and the weeds to grow together until the time of harvest. He does that not because He is too weak to assert Himself, but because He is too wise to assert Himself.

C. S. Lewis said it rather interestingly in his book *Mere Christianity*. He first described how God seems to be operating a secret society on earth in an enemy territory. Then he asks these questions:

Why is God landing in this enemy-occupied world in disguise and starting a sort of secret society to undermine the devil? Why is He not landing in force, invading it? Is it that He isn't strong enough? Well, Christians think He's going to land in force; we do not know when. But we can guess why He is delaying. He wants to give us the chance of joining His side freely. I do not suppose that you and I would have thought much of a Frenchman who waited till the Allies were marching into Germany and then announced he was on our side. God will invade. But I wonder whether people who asked God to interfere directly and openly in our world quite realize what it will be like when He does. When that happens, it is the end of the world. When the author walks on to the stage the play is over. God is going to invade, all right: but what is the good of saying you're on His side then, when you see the whole natural universe melting away like a dream and something else—something it never entered your head to conceive—comes crashing in; something so beautiful to some of us and so terrible to others that none of us will have any choice left? For this time it will be God without disguise; something so overwhelming that it will strike either irresistible love or irresistible horror into every creature. It will be too late then to choose your side. There's no use saying you choose to lie down when it has become impossible to stand up. That will not be the time for choosing: it will be the time when we discover which side we really have chosen, whether we realized it before or not. Now, today, this moment, is our chance to choose the right side. God is holding back to give us that chance. It will not last for ever. We must take it or leave it.[2]

My friend, I invite you to join me today in the determination to continue to trust the One who knows how to handle the wheat and the weeds in the world, in the church, and in your heart. Then one day soon you will stand with the group of people on the sea that looks like glass, and you will sing a song from your heart that goes something like this:

"Great and marvelous are your deeds,
Lord God Almighty.
Just and true are your ways,
King of the ages.
Who will not fear you, O Lord,
and bring glory to your name?
For you alone are holy.
All nations will come and worship before you,
for your righteous acts have been revealed"
(Revelation 15:3, 4).

In the meantime, aren't you thankful for the way He stays with all of us till the harvest?

1. Ellen G. White, *Christ's Object Lessons* (Nampa, Idaho: Pacific Press®, 1952), 71.
2. C. S. Lewis, *Mere Christianity* (New York: The Macmillan Company, 1952), 65, 66.

Chapter 6

You Can't Be Forgiven Unless You Forgive

I teach a class called the Dynamics of Christian Living. One day a student asked, "Would it be possible to flunk this class and still go to heaven?" Another student reversed the question and asked, "Would it be possible to get an A in this class and go to the other place?"

I had opportunity to ponder these questions one day. A student who had taken the class and had gotten an A went to live with some of my parishioners. He didn't seem to think it was necessary to pay his rent. When my church members decided that it was time for the student to move to other accommodations, the student took several expensive items from the house and moved to another state.

When I heard the story, I asked the people what they were doing to bring the student to justice. They said, "Nothing. What can you do when someone has moved out of state?" I was so upset about the situation that I thought maybe I could write to this student and tell him that unless he made this right, I would change his grade from an A to an F. Maybe that would help!

Jesus told a story about the kingdom that is similar to this episode:

"The kingdom of heaven is like a king who wanted to settle accounts with his servants. As he began the settlement, a man who owed him ten thousand talents was brought to him. Since he was not able to pay, the master ordered that he and his wife and his children and all that he had be sold to repay the debt.

"The servant fell on his knees before him. 'Be patient with me,' he begged, 'and I will pay back everything.' The servant's master took pity on him, canceled the debt and let him go.

"But when that servant went out, he found one of his fellow servants who owed him a hundred denarii. He grabbed him and began to choke him. 'Pay back what you owe me!' he demanded.

"His fellow servant fell to his knees and begged him, 'Be patient with me, and I will pay you back.'

"But he refused. Instead, he went off and had the man thrown into prison until he could pay the debt. When the other servants saw what had happened, they were greatly distressed and went and told their master everything that had happened.

"Then the master called the servant in. 'You wicked servant,' he said, 'I canceled all that debt of yours because you begged me to. Shouldn't you have had mercy on your fellow servant just as I had on you?' In anger his master turned him over to the jailers to be tortured, until he should pay back all he owed.

"This is how my heavenly Father will treat each of you unless you forgive your brother from your heart" (Matthew 18:23-35).

IS THE KING TRUSTWORTHY?

Would you be willing to trust this king? Do you think he is a good king? You may say, "It depends on who I am in the story."

All right, who *are* you in the story?

If you're the one who went to the king and told on the unforgiving servant, then you're a man of action like the king. He took care of the problem right away.

If you're the man who owed the hundred pence, you're like the king. You're glad to see your tormenter behind bars. You think the king is fair and just.

But if you're the one who owed the ten thousand talents and thought you'd escaped prison, you probably are not too happy with the king, isn't that right?

And then Jesus says, "This is the way My Father is going to treat you." Sounds like a pretty severe God, complete with hellfire and brimstone, doesn't it? Would you like to be delivered to the tormenters by such a king?

This is a hard parable. The meaning is not on the surface. But as we attempt to grapple with it, let's back up two verses to what came just before. Peter and Jesus were talking: "Peter came to Jesus and asked, 'Lord, how many times shall I forgive my brother when he sins against me? Up to seven times?' "

Don't you like Peter? He was always out in front, opening his mouth before he knew what he was going to say! He thought he had come up with a good idea here. The Pharisees limited forgiveness to three times—sort of a forgiveness ball game: three strikes and you're out. Peter had doubled their number and then added one for good measure, making seven, the perfect number. And he was all ready for Jesus to respond, "Why bless you, Peter, what a beautiful thought!"

Instead, Jesus suggested that he multiply seven by seventy! Obviously, He was recommending unlimited forgiveness. Then Jesus tells the story of a man who owes the equivalent of $20 million. He's forgiven, but he refuses to forgive another man who owes him about $30. So the king throws the forgiven debtor into prison. And Jesus says, "This is what My Father is like."

Seems incongruous, doesn't it? But let's examine it more closely and try to find the truth that Jesus was presenting.

The drama of this story really comes in three parts. Let's look at each part separately.

Part 1—The $20 Million Debt. This man owes $20 million, and Jesus said he didn't have the wherewithal to pay. Well, of course! How many of us could pay that kind of money? But the man doesn't realize his desperate condition. He falls down before the king, crying, "Be patient with me, and I will pay back everything."

Now, either he is a fool, or he is trying to con the king. He pretends to worship the king, but in reality, he's worshiping himself. He thinks that somehow he's big enough to pay his debt. And in this parable, which is really a parable about salvation, the man realizes neither the enormity of his debt nor his helplessness to pay it.

Are you in debt? Oh, I'm not talking about the house payment and the car payment and the gas and electricity and tuition for the kids in school. The apostle Paul put it this way in Romans 1: "I am a debtor." He was talking about the debt we owe to Jesus, the debt we can never repay.

When we come before the King, how foolish we would be to say, "Be patient with me, and I will pay." We can't pay. We're in debt to Jesus, and we don't have even one dime to put toward our account.

The man in the parable is offered forgiveness for his debt. The king forgave him. But there's something important that we need to begin noticing here. Forgiveness is a two-way street. To be forgiven, we have to accept the forgiveness that has been offered. The offer of forgiveness is not enough.

There have been times in the history of our legal system when people were awarded pardons but refused to accept them. The first time it happened, the authorities had to do some discussion and consideration before they knew how to handle it. They concluded that if someone refuses a pardon, then that person isn't pardoned after all. It's as simple as that!

How do we know the man in the parable didn't accept the pardon? Because of his reaction! How would you react if someone were to come to you today and say, "All of your debts are canceled as of right now. You don't owe anything anymore." Would you walk away without even saying thank you? The evidence in the story is that the man didn't even do that. He just walked away.

Part II—The $30 Debt. The first thing the $20-million debtor did, instead of falling at the feet of the king in gratitude and love, was to go out and nail one of his fellow servants, a man who owed him a paltry $30. He threatened him, and even when this second servant offered the same plea the first one had just made before the king, the heart of the $20-million debtor was not softened. He had his fellow servant thrown into prison.

Why did he do this? Maybe he was simply greedy, and although he was glad to have the weight of the $20 million off his back, he thought this would be a good chance to get some pocket money to celebrate with! But there's another possibility. If he hadn't really accepted the king's offer of pardon, then perhaps he was intending to recoup his resources and pay the king what he owed. Maybe he didn't like charity. Maybe he was determined not to be indebted to the king. Maybe he didn't want to live with the sense of obligation that the forgiveness might give him.

This man had a long, hard winter ahead if he was going to repay the $20-million debt thirty dollars at a time! The ratio of the debts was several hundred thousand to one. So he had a lot of hard labor ahead of him. But whatever his motive, one fact is clear. He didn't treat his fellow servant as the king had treated him.

Part III—He's in the Jail House Now! There seems to be a code in most schools, and perhaps in most of the world as well, that it is not cool to snitch on someone. Young people have a particularly strong code of ethics that says you don't tell, you don't squeal, you don't fink—or whatever the current term for it is. They have all kinds of labels for it, none of them complimentary! Tattling is considered an almost unforgivable sin.

But either the code of ethics in the court of this king was different or perhaps there are some things that are so blatant, so bad, that you can't help but go and tell. Anyway, some of the servants told the king what had happened, and the king was angry. He called the first man back into his presence, sentenced him to prison, and delivered him to the tormenters (the devil and his angels) until he paid his debt.

There are those today who don't want a God who gets angry. But this king was angry. They don't want a God who is active in judgment. But this king sent his servant to prison, to the tormenters. He didn't just *allow* him to experience the results of his wrongdoing. He moved in and brought the results to bear. And it says the debtor was to stay in the prison until he had paid all his debt. That was going to take a while, wasn't it? What a strange story!

CONTRAST BETWEEN THE TWO KINGDOMS

One thing we can learn from this story is that there are two kingdoms, the kingdom of heaven and the kingdom of this world.

And their method of operation is strikingly different. In the kingdom of this world, you get what you earn, and you earn what you get. You work your way. We don't know a whole lot about forgiveness and gifts and mercy in this kingdom in which we live.

People have struggled with this difference. And when they understand that the kingdom of heaven is on the gift system and that merit and earning and wages and credit are not part of that kingdom, they find it hard to grasp.

In the kingdom of heaven, we are freely forgiven, and, in turn we are to forgive freely. There is no forgiveness available for the one who is unforgiving toward others. But that poses a problem. Is it our willingness to forgive that causes God to forgive us? There's a line in the Lord's Prayer that says, "Forgive us our debts *as* we forgive our debtors." It doesn't say, "Forgive us *because* we forgive." Does that help your understanding of this story? Or do you have trouble understanding the difference between *because* and *as*?

Let's look at two possible solutions. You may decide for yourself which category you think this man belongs in, but there seems to be two possibilities to account for someone who has been forgiven becoming unforgiving.

The first, as we have already mentioned, is to never accept forgiveness in the first place. Forgiveness always requires two parties. If there has been a break in our relationship, either between someone else and us or between God and us, both parties must become willing for reconciliation to take place. Otherwise there will be no reconciliation.

Have you ever, in your human relationships, found yourself estranged from someone you loved? Have you offered forgiveness and had it refused? When that happens, even if you were in the right, the relationship dies.

When Jesus died on the cross, He made it possible for forgiveness to be offered to everybody—regardless of who we are or what we've done or where we come from. Because of Jesus, we can be forgiven. It doesn't matter whether we owe $20 million or only $30. Forgiveness is offered freely to every person.

But as beautiful as that is, it isn't worth a dime to me unless I am willing to accept it. So if I haven't accepted the forgiveness the King has extended, then the time of judgment and the going to prison is inevitable.

I don't believe this man ever accepted the king's forgiveness. There was no evidence of appreciation, there is evidence he was still intent on repayment, and there is evidence he didn't know what forgiveness was all about by the way he treated his fellow servant.

Another possible interpretation of this parable says that it is possible for people to be truly forgiven and yet end up not forgiving their brother. Here's how that can happen: People may have once received forgiveness but subsequently become unmerciful because they've turned away from God's pardoning love. They've separated themselves from God and are in the same condition as before they were forgiven. If all that was needed was to accept God's forgiveness once and then automatically, forever after, people are forgiving, there would be no need for the warning inherent in this story, as well as in the Lord's Prayer.

We might call this the "so long as" principle. So long as we are connected to God and depending on Him, sin has no power over us. It makes no difference what sin we're talking about. As soon as we separate from God and His control, we're in the same condition as before we were forgiven. The religion of Christ is based on relationship, never behavior. When we come to Christ in the first place, He forgives our sins and all our bad behavior is forgotten. But if we choose to separate from Christ, all our good behavior is of no value! Ezekiel 3:20 talks about that.

The simple truth is that if we are connected to Christ and under His control, we *will be* forgiving toward others. And if we break from that dependence, we *will not be* forgiving. The unforgiving spirit is not the cause; it is the result of having separated from God.

This is inherent in the passage. Notice, it is not enough to *act* as if you are forgiving. What does it say? It says this is what God will do to you "unless you forgive your brother *from your heart"* (emphasis supplied).

The only way we can forgive from the heart is if we have had our hearts broken and subdued by the Spirit of God. It's not something we can work on ourselves. It's not something we offer to God—rather, it is something He offers to us. And it is ours *so long as* we accept it.

Are you still nervous about the angry king? Just remember—it doesn't say at whom he was angry. It just says he was angry—presumably with his unforgiving servant. But there is another way to look at the king's wrath. God has always been angry at sin. He hates it, doesn't He? He is always angry at the deception in His universe that would lead His own creation to separate from Him and die. Don't you want God to be angry with that?

But you can still see a God who chokes with tears as He considers one who has walked away from Him. He is eternally committed to allowing us to choose freely. But we will never be able to understand the depth of the pain that comes to His great heart of love when we choose against Him. God's heart is broken anew each time He offers reconciliation and pardon and one of His children refuses to accept them.

We cannot pay the debt we owe God. We cannot pay one penny of it. All we can do is to bow at His feet and say, "Jesus paid it all, all to Him I owe." And the debt of love that we owe is as big as all eternity.

Chapter 7

The Light That Blinds

Have you ever closed your eyes and wondered what it's like to be blind? Have you ever wondered what it's like to have been born blind? Maybe that would be easier. And then to be given your sight—how would you orient yourself if that happened? You'd be wondering what it was all about.

For some reason when I was a little child I was afraid of blind people. I've tried to figure out why. Was there some dramatic experience that programmed me to be frightened of blind people? My father used to get Pierce Knox, a very talented blind musician, to come and do concerts for his evangelistic meetings. And I was frightened to death of Pierce Knox.

When Jesus was here, His heart got carried away on occasions, and He healed even without being asked. We see this in today's story, which is in a sense a real-life parable, a real-life parable of something that goes deeper than mere physical blindness. The real issues in John 9 are two kinds of people passing on the road. One kind is going down, and the other is going up. One group is being given their sight, while the other is becoming blind, spiritually.

We'll take a look at this story in its entirety. Let's start right at the beginning, and we'll pause here and there to consider some major texts. It is interesting to note that John is the only one who records this story. He does it for the deep spiritual meaning.

> As he [Jesus] went along, he saw a man blind from birth. His disciples asked him, "Rabbi, who sinned, this man or his parents, that he was born blind?" [Wrong question!] "Neither this man nor his parents sinned," said Jesus, "but this happened so that the work of God might be displayed in his life" (John 9:1).

At the surface, it sounds like these are the first people who never sinned. But the last I checked, both this man and his parents were sinners and had sinned. Jesus didn't explain, but He was saying that this man's blindness was not caused by someone's sin—although he *was* blind because someone sinned "way back when," as we know.

We need to pause here, right off the top in this story, because this is a common question. It still hangs on today. People who go through some terrible affliction or handicap or disease often find it easy to ask the same question: Who goofed? And it would be easy for us to hold up this story and say that people's suffering never results from their sins. But, yes, it does. Jesus is not making a blanket statement here that the law of the harvest never works. We know that if people choose to smoke, they're likely to face death by lung cancer. We know that this is the result of sin. What sin? The sin of not accepting the Bible's pronouncement that our bodies are temples of the Holy Spirit (see 1 Corinthians 6:19). So we know that there are consequences to our wrong choices. One of the most terrible diseases that is spreading everywhere today is very much the result, as a rule, of people's sins. We need to realize that the story of the blind man is the exception to the rule. The law of the harvest is very real.

I have admired Elder A. G. Daniels, who I believe served as General Conference president as long as, if not longer than, anyone else. He was convicted by the pen of inspiration that he should encourage our people to stop eating meat. Really? Yes! So, they could get to heaven? No, no!—but because it had been revealed to the inspired messenger that cancer was largely caused by eating flesh foods, eating meat.[1] Her purpose in trying to get our world leader to deal with this meat-eating issue and to encourage people to do the same was for their health and their long life and their happiness, not in order for them to get to heaven. A. G. Daniels refused to do it, though. Finally, as he was dying of cancer, the brethren came around and tried to get him to allow them to have a special prayer and anointing. He said, "No, I will not do it. I made my own choice, and I will bear the consequences of my own choice." Very interesting! There often is a definite relationship between what we do and what we experience as a result of what we do.

In this parable, however, this man was born blind, and I am very thankful that I don't have to join the disciples in asking, "Who goofed?" I will never forget what a relief it was to discover, after we found out we had a handicapped child, that this was not the wages of someone's sin. This was the result of a world gone wrong, a world of sin, and the wages of sin is the second death, period. We all experience the results of a world gone wrong; as the popular saying goes, "Into each life some rain must fall"—and into some more than others. We all experience the result of being born on the wrong planet. So, our bad experiences are not always the immediate result of someone having sinned, though they can be.

TRUTH PERVERTED

The classic book on the life of Christ, *The Desire of Ages*, offers some real help on this issue. Here is what it says:

> It was generally believed by the Jews that sin is punished in this life. Every affliction was regarded as the penalty of some wrongdoing, either of the sufferer himself or of his parents. It is true that all suffering results from the transgression of God's law, but this truth had become perverted. Satan, the author of sin and all its results, had led men to look upon disease and death as proceeding from God,—as punishment arbitrarily inflicted on account of sin. Hence one upon whom some great affliction or calamity had fallen had the additional burden of being regarded as a great sinner.
>
> Thus the way was prepared for the Jews to reject Jesus. He who "hath borne our griefs, and carried our sorrows" was looked upon by the Jews as "stricken, smitten of God, and afflicted;" and they hid their faces from Him (Isaiah 53:4, 3).
>
> God had given a lesson designed to prevent this. The history of Job had shown that suffering is inflicted by Satan, and is overruled by God for purposes of mercy. But Israel did not understand the lesson. The same error for which God had reproved the friends of Job was repeated by the Jews in their rejection of Christ.
>
> The belief of the Jews in regard to the relation of sin and suffering was held by Christ's disciples. While Jesus

corrected their error, He did not explain the cause of the man's affliction, but told them what would be the result.[2]

Herein is a good reason for pause. We see affliction on every side, and we know what will be the result one day soon. When Jesus comes again and we sing "Face to face with Christ my Savior" for real, what a wonderful tribute to the power and kindness of God it will be when sin, sickness, pain, disease, and death are history. We won't have to spend our time figuring out who goofed. We can spend meaningful time rejoicing when the tables turn and it's all over.

In essence, Jesus said to His disciples, "You're now going to see the power of God displayed in this man's life." His heart and His feelings got carried away, and He moved in on the blind man without even being asked. Scripture tells us that He said, "As long as it is day, we must do the work of him who sent me. Night is coming, when no one can work. While I am in the world, I am the light of the world." Then it says, "Having said this, he spit on the ground, made some mud with the saliva, and put it on the man's eyes" (verses 4-6).

Huh? That's kind of crude! I'm tempted to spend some time on that. If you had been the blind man, would you have said, "No, thanks. I don't want any of that"? I've heard people speculate on that. From the same inspired source: "It was evident that there was no healing virtue in the clay, or in the pool wherein the blind man was sent to wash, but that the virtue was in Christ."[3] So, we don't have some kind of heavenly spit here. We don't have some magic place where people can go and get their healing. Jesus had a purpose in what He did that someday we may understand better.

" 'Go,' he told him, 'wash in the Pool of Siloam' [which means Sent]. So the man went and washed and came home seeing" (John

9:7). A blind man who has never seen before can now see. What does that feel like? "His neighbors and those who had formerly seen him begging asked, 'Isn't this the same man who used to sit and beg?' Some claimed that he was. Others said, 'No, he only looks like him' " (verses 8, 9). Evidently his countenance changed when he could see.

"He himself insisted, 'I am the man.' 'How then were your eyes opened?' they demanded. He replied, 'The man they call Jesus made some mud and put it on my eyes. He told me to go to Siloam and wash. So I went and washed, and then I could see' " (verses 9-11).

"The *man* they call Jesus . . ." This is the first indication we have of this poor blind man's recognition of Jesus. "He is a man. He did such and such, and now I can see."

" 'Where is this man?' they asked him. 'I don't know,' he said" (verse 12).

Interesting! Have you ever had Jesus do something for you and you knew He did, only to be discouraged later and feel that you don't even know where He is? Maybe you have had times in your life when you have wondered where Jesus was—but you know He has done something special for you nonetheless.

SABBATH BREAKERS?

In the next part of the story, the blind man is brought to the Pharisees (verse 13). The day on which Jesus made the clay and opened the blind man's eyes was the Sabbath. This is the fifth time that Jesus made the mistake of healing someone on the Sabbath day. Bad move, Lord. You should be more politically astute. But Jesus did this on purpose. In fact, He might have done the spitting, mixing, making mud, having the blind man walk to the Pool of Siloam, and all the rest of it, because it *was* the Sabbath. He wanted to get their attention and show them that even though He ran the risk of being charged with Sabbath breaking, people were more important than the petty rules that some people had manufactured.

When the blind man was brought to the Pharisees, they too asked him how he had been healed:

> Therefore the Pharisees also asked him how he had received his sight. "He put mud on my eyes," the man replied, "and I washed, and now I see."
>
> Some of the Pharisees said, "This man is not from God, for he does not keep the Sabbath." But others asked, "How can a sinner do such miraculous signs?" So they were divided. Finally they turned again to the blind man, "What have you to say about him? It was your eyes he opened." The man replied, "He is a prophet" (verses 15-17).

Insight number one, for the blind man, was that Jesus is a man. Insight number two: He is a prophet. This man is beginning to be a believer. You'd find it hard not to be a believer if what happened to him would happen to you.

"The Jews still did not believe that he had been blind and had received his sight until they sent for the man's parents. 'Is this your son?' they asked. 'Is this the one you say was born blind? How is it that now he can see?' " (verse 19).

Three questions. The parents answered two:

> "We know he is our son," the parents answered, "and we know he was born blind. But how he can see now, or who opened his eyes, we don't know. Ask him. He is of age; he will speak for himself." His parents said this because they were afraid of the Jews, for already the Jews had de-

cided that anyone who acknowledged that Jesus was the
Christ would be put out of the synagogue. That was why
his parents said, "He is of age; ask him" (verses 20-22).

So, now we see this poor man isolated and totally abandoned.
We're not sure how many friends he had before, but now even his
family, in a sense, abandons him. And they call him again. He
stands before the religious prelates. " 'Give glory to God,' they said.
'We know this man is a sinner.' He replied, 'Whether he is a sinner
or not, I don't know. One thing I do know. I was blind but now I
see!' " (verse 25).

Not bad! I've always been intrigued by that response. Aren't
you? "If you want a theological discussion, go ahead," he says,
"have a good time. Right now, I'm having a good time. I'm seeing.
Whereas I was blind, now I see."

It reminds me of a time we were faced with a devil-possessed
girl at Pacific Union College, and the dean said to me, "Can you
do something?"

I said, "Well, what is it? Is this drugs? Is this mental illness? Do
you know anything about her? Do you know the difference between mental illness and devil possession?"

He said, "You want a theological discussion?"

I went, "Whooow!"

"Then they asked him, 'What did he do to you? How did he
open your eyes?' He answered, 'I have told you already and you
did not listen. Why do you want to hear it again? Do you want to
become his disciples, too?' " (verses 26, 27).

Insight number three: This man is becoming a disciple of Jesus.
"Do you want to become his disciples, too?" he asks.

Well, this was the wrong thing to say to these proud religious
leaders. "Then they hurled insults at him and said, 'You are this

fellow's disciple! We are disciples of Moses! We know that God spoke to Moses, but as for this fellow, we don't even know where he comes from" (verses 28, 29).

Now notice the response of this poor, illiterate, uneducated blind man, who could only sit by the side of the road and sell pencils or walk across the intersection with his white cane going, "Tap, tap, tap":

> The man answered, "Now that is remarkable! You don't know where he comes from, yet he opened my eyes. We know that God does not listen to sinners. He listens to the godly man who does his will. Nobody has ever heard of opening the eyes of a man born blind. If this man were not from God, he could do nothing" (verses 30-33).

Insight number four: Now he is acknowledging that Jesus is God. That was too much for the religious leaders. "To this they replied, 'You were steeped in sin at birth; how dare you lecture us!' And they threw him out" (verse 34).

OUR SOURCE OF WISDOM

You have to admit that the wisdom that Jesus had from above was demonstrated in the life of a poor, illiterate blind man. And we have the same source of wisdom. When we are called before prelates, whether now or later, we can give the same kind of profound answers, because the God who was responsible for the blind man's healing was also responsible for his speech. He was able to put these proud religious leaders in their place because God was at work.

"Jesus heard that they had cast him out. And when he had found him . . ." (verse 35). Notice that Jesus went looking for him;

He heard that he was abandoned. Jesus had a heart not only to heal him, but also to bring comfort.

> He said, "Do you believe in the Son of Man?" "Who is he, sir?" the man asked. "Tell me so that I may believe in him." Jesus replied, "You have now seen him. In fact, he is the one speaking with you." Then the man said, "*Lord,* [here is his final insight] I believe." And he worshipped him (verse 35-38, emphasis supplied).

Watch this man go from darkness to light. Watch this man as the insights come. First, "Jesus is a man." Next, "He is a prophet. Then, "I am one of his disciples." "He is of God." "He *is* God." And finally, "Lord, I trust You," and he worships Him. At the same time the religious leaders were going into darkness, into blindness. They crossed paths on the road, headed in opposite directions. Tragic!

I wonder what the blind man saw when he saw Jesus. Did he see a medieval Christ who looked more like a ghost? Or ugly, as the medieval sculptures portray him. When we read that Jesus was a man of sorrow and acquainted with grief, that He had no comeliness that we should desire Him, does this mean that He was not good looking at all? Whatever the blind man saw must have been the most beautiful Person that he would ever see. And he said, "Lord, I believe," and he worshiped Him.

Now comes the final crunch. "Jesus said, 'for judgment I have come into this world, so that the blind will see and those who see will become blind' " (verse 39). The main thrust of John 9 is the difference between light and darkness. Some people go toward the light; some people go into darkness, spiritually.

I once came across something that startled me. Basically, it was the thought that all we have to do to come under Satan's control is to knowingly turn away from just one point of truth. That's all. To come under conviction concerning one point of truth and deliberately turn away makes one liable to Satan's control. If that doesn't send us to our knees and make us pray the prayer of the song, "Open mine eyes that I may see," what else would?

"Some Pharisees who were with him heard him say this and asked, 'What? Are we blind too?' Jesus said, 'If you were blind, you would not be guilty of sin; but now that you claim you can see, your guilt remains' " (verses 40, 41).

Do you have light that you are grateful for? Do you have light that you have pondered and wondered about? What are you doing with it? Are you coming into greater light and greater insight, like the poor blind man? Or are you joining the religious leaders, headed toward darkness? It's a worthwhile question.

It's a terrible thing to do to a man who has been blind all of his life—to heal him. Can you imagine what he is faced with now? No education. He can't sit by the side of the street and sell pencils anymore. What's he going to do for a living? His family has essentially abandoned him. He's alone.

Maybe you too have felt alone. But God has a plan for everyone's life, including yours. The same God who healed this poor blind man proved before the prelates that He would be with him the rest of his days. And we can be assured that the Jesus toward whose light we travel will be with us all our days.

---

1. See Ellen G. White, *Testimonies for the Church* (Nampa, Idaho: Pacific Press®, 1948), 9:159.
2. Ellen G. White, *The Desire of Ages* (Nampa, Idaho: Pacific Press®, 1940), 471.
3. Ibid.

Chapter 8

Jesus, the Good Samaritan

I am a gambler. Oh, I don't mean the kind who spends Sundays at the local gambling hall. But I find it challenging to try to make it to the next town with my car's gas gauge on empty! My family does not particularly appreciate my gambling instinct, so when they are with me, they have a way of controlling this propensity. But believe it or not, through this "vegetarian" form of gambling I have met many nice people. Perhaps it could even be considered a form of witnessing!

One day I was cooling my heels by the side of a highway off-ramp in California. The people in the Lincoln Continentals went by, and so did the people wearing the business suits. The people with fancy vans went past, and the Winnebagos as well. Then along came a young man with long hair and a beard, driving a battered pickup. He stopped, and not only did he take me to get gas, but he also brought me back and made sure my car was going before he went on his way. I've thought a lot about that experience since that time. Good Samaritans are sometimes surprising kinds of people, aren't they?

The story of the original good Samaritan is an old, old story, but let's look at it. Maybe we can find something new. Jesus gave a mini-parable in Matthew 13:52, about things old and new. "He said to them, 'Therefore every teacher of the law who has been instructed about the kingdom of heaven is like the owner of a house who brings out of his storeroom new treasures as well as old.' "

That's one of the exciting things about the kingdom of heaven. It's not possible to exhaust the supply of treasure. We understand that even throughout eternity we will be studying things old and new. And sometimes it is the new twist that brings a breakthrough to people, who see truth they hadn't noticed before. Every new disclosure of the Savior's love turns the balance for some soul in one direction or the other. So let's look for the old and new in the story of the good Samaritan.

A TRAP FOR JESUS

The Jewish leaders were out to get Jesus, so they engaged one of their champions, a sharp lawyer, to try to trip Him up. They had hopes that with his fine, argumentative mind, he could get Jesus out on thin ice and then sink Him. The one thing they failed to allow for was that this lawyer they sent to trap Jesus was a sincere seeker for truth himself. He had been watching Jesus, and he was glad for an excuse to initiate personal contact for his own sake.

So, this "expert in the law stood up to test Jesus. 'Teacher,' he asked, 'what must I do to inherit eternal life?' " (Luke 10:25). This was typical of the religion of his day, and it's still typical today. Human nature hasn't changed. Even most Christians think of the Christian life in terms of doing rather than in terms of knowing. One of the truths that Jesus came to present was that the Christian life and eternal life are not based upon what we do; they are based upon whom we know. Jesus said, "This is eternal life: that they may know you, the only true God, and Jesus Christ, whom you have sent" (John 17:3). The Christian life, then, is not based on behavior, but on relationship.

You might expect Jesus to go straight into a discourse on our relationship with God. Instead, He asked the lawyer, "What is written in the Law? . . . How do you read it?"

Sounds like a legalistic answer, doesn't it?

The lawyer responded in kind: " ' "Love the Lord your God with all your heart and with all your soul and with all your strength and with all your mind" and, "Love your neighbor as yourself." ' "

" 'You have answered correctly,' Jesus replied. 'Do this and you will live' " (verses 27, 28).

As you know, if you have studied Jesus' method of teaching, He was not in the habit of giving pat answers. He knew, as the Master Teacher, that the way to teach is to lead the student into an atmosphere where he can discover for himself. Jesus answered the lawyer's first question by asking him another question. He held His ground. He was leading this man to discover truth for himself, in a novel way, in a way that he would remember.

The lawyer found himself rattling off the answer to his own question like a school kid reciting, and apparently he was embarrassed. This wasn't working out the way he had anticipated. So he tried again to take the discussion to an intellectual plane where he could compete. He came up with another question: "But he wanted to justify himself, so he asked Jesus, 'And who is my neighbor?' " (verse 29).

This question was a common one in those days. The Jewish people were not exactly neighborly. In fact, they were known to be quite exclusive. They had long discussions about whom they should associate with and whom they should avoid, and the list of people to avoid was always the longer one.

Jesus responded to the lawyer's question by telling a story:

"A man was going down from Jerusalem to Jericho, when he fell into the hands of robbers. They stripped him of his clothes, beat him and went away, leaving him half dead. A priest happened to be going down the same road, and when he saw the man, he passed by on the other side. So too, a Levite, when he came to the place and saw him, passed by on the other side. But a Samaritan, as he traveled, came where the man was; and when he saw him, he took pity on him. He went to him and bandaged his wounds, pouring on oil and wine. Then he put the man on his own donkey, took him to an inn and took care of him [apparently all night]. The next day he took out two silver coins and gave them to the innkeeper. 'Look after him,' he said, 'and when I return, I will reimburse you for any extra expenses you may have.' "

Then Jesus asked the lawyer, " 'Which of these three do you think was a neighbor to the man who fell into the hands of robbers?'

"The expert in the law replied, 'The one who had mercy on him.' [He didn't want to use the word *Samaritan*.]

"Jesus told him, 'Go and do likewise.' " End of story.

Was that really the end of the story? Do you hear a story like the one about the good Samaritan and find yourself able to go and do likewise? Or was Jesus sending this lawyer to his knees?

Good Samaritans aren't made by starting a Good Samaritan Club and deliberately choosing to be compassionate. Instead, they are Good Samaritans because they can't help it. This lawyer, who could not even take the name *Samaritan* on his lips, could become loving and compassionate only by going to his knees and becoming acquainted with the One whom Jesus represented.

PUT YOURSELF IN THE PICTURE

The best way to personalize a Bible story such as this is to put yourself in the picture. When you read about the thief on the cross, *you're* the thief on the cross. When you read about blind Bartimaeus by the side of the road, *you're* the blind person crying out, "Jesus, son of David, have mercy on me." So when you study the story of the good Samaritan, *you're* the good Samaritan . . . No, you're not! And I'm not either! At worst, we're the ones who beat him up in the first place. At best, we're the one who was beaten up.

So, you are the man traveling from Jerusalem to Jericho. It's a trip of about twenty miles. Jerusalem stands at a higher elevation, so you are walking downhill. You walk briskly, for this is not a safe place to loiter. This is a place that has recesses and caves, where thieves and robbers lurk and frequently waylay travelers, as you well know.

You go down through a narrow ravine known as the Valley of Blood, and the inevitable happens. A group of armed men attack you from behind. You haven't even a chance to defend yourself. They take your money and your watch and even your clothes. And then, as if that were not enough, they beat you and finally leave you unconscious, weltering in your own blood.

You lie there for a long time. Finally you come to. The sun is hot. You try to move but find you can't get up. You groan and struggle, but it's no use. However, there's good news. You see the preacher coming. Surely the preacher will help. But he doesn't even slow down. He passes by on the other side of the road and barely glances in your direction.

Don't be too hard on the preacher. He may have been scheduled to deliver a sermon at the synagogue in Jericho and was running late. Maybe he was even planning to preach on brotherly love. If he hung around the Valley of Blood, where robbers had already done someone in, the same thing might happen to him. It would certainly be the lesser of two evils to leave you and hurry on to Jericho. Shouldn't the spiritual need of his parishioners take priority over the needs of one person who was probably going to die anyway? Surely the priest must have done some rationalizing like this as he hurried on his way.

You're getting chilled now. The sun has gone down behind an outcropping of rock, and you lie in the shadows. You're afraid it's all over for you, for not many travelers are on the road at this time of day. But good news: Here comes the church treasurer! Not only can he help you to safety, but perhaps he can even pay for your medical bills and even get you some clothes. Hope rises in your heart as you see him come over to where you are.

You try to speak, but your words come out as a groan. Your lips are parched; you can hardly move. He looks down at you and then glances quickly around to see if robbers are lurking nearby. And then he hurries on toward town.

Of course he must hurry on—he's carrying a bag filled with the offering money. It wouldn't be right to risk losing the Lord's money by staying in a place like this. Furthermore, his wife and children are expecting him, and running the risk of getting beaten up and robbed on the Jericho Road would not be the fatherly thing to do. He must have thought it through carefully as he hurried on his way, pausing now and again to glance back over his shoulder to make sure he wasn't being followed.

It looks hopeless now. You struggle again to move but find you are too weak. The attempt leaves you dizzy and short of breath. It's almost dark, and you are chilled to the bone. You try to resign yourself to slowly losing consciousness and giving in to the inevitable. Even if another traveler were to come this way, you wouldn't likely be seen there, off the side of the road in the shadows.

But you hear footsteps, and you strain your eyes to see who's approaching—and your heart sinks. Oh! It's a Samaritan. You know how things are between the Jews and the Samaritans. You know how you've treated Samaritans in the past. And you shrink back inside yourself, knowing that if your roles were reversed, not only would you not help him, you would probably spit in his face.

The Samaritan slows down. He sees you, and you brace yourself for the worst. But he speaks gently to you. "What happened? You're hurt! Let me help you." You can't believe it! He touches you, carefully examining you so as to cause you the least pain possible. He begins to bind up your wounds, pouring on oil and wine. He feels your clammy skin and realizes how cold you are. He takes off his own coat, in spite of the coolness of the evening, and wraps you in its warmth. And then kindly and tenderly he helps you onto his donkey and takes you to the closest inn, all the while encouraging you to hope for a full recovery.

As you sink back into the warmth and comfort of the bed provided for you at the good Samaritan's expense, you can hardly believe your good fortune. He cares for you all through the long night, and in the morning, when you are feeling stronger, you hear him make arrangements for you to rest there as long as necessary—*at his expense!* You think about your family and friends and know they will never believe it when you tell them—but you can hardly wait to share the good news of what happened to you on the road to Jericho.

Let's redo the story now, with the most exciting part, because this is the story of Jesus. Long ago, the father of our race went down—way down. He went down from a garden with two trees, and his wife went with him. They went down, and the race has been going down ever since, degenerating in physical strength, mental power, and moral worth. The thief and robber who stripped them of their garments of light had gone down before them, down from the heavenly courts. He wounded them and left them for dead. The wounded victims tried to stitch fig leaves together to replace the garments he had taken from them, but it didn't work. And the human race is still on that downward path.

Then the Good Samaritan came. By chance? No, He planned it. He came on purpose. He saw us and had pity on us. He left His home, the safety of His beautiful home, to come down to this world of trouble. He is touched with the feelings of our infirmities. He put His robe around us, sacrificing His own life to save ours. He poured oil and wine on our wounds—the oil of the Holy Spirit and the wine of His own shed blood. With His stripes we are healed.

And then He took us to the inn. Do you know where it is? There's one in your town! It may be a simple building, or it may have steeples and stained glass. But it's there. And He gives instruction to the innkeepers. If you haven't found yourself in the story yet, you'd better now! For He says to the innkeepers, "Take care of this person, and when I come again, I will repay you."

And now you are one of the innkeepers! The Good Samaritan doesn't just stop by once and then disappear. He's coming back! And He's promised, "When I come again, I will repay you."

Chapter 9

The Prodigal Sons

He lived in his father's house through his growing-up years. Now all of that seemed long ago. Once he had been a trusting child who held on to his father's hand as they walked out to do the chores, looked at his father with love and respect, and found joy in companionship with his father. But slowly, almost imperceptibly, he had changed. Now he resented his father's restraints, chafed at his counsel, and detested his instructions. He thought his father was severe, exacting, unreasonable. For a time he lived as a prodigal at home, but now he wanted out. Finally, one day he came up with a plan.

He went to his father and boldly asked for his share of the inheritance. He knew he would need these blessings in order to make it comfortably on his own. He wasn't foolish enough to simply run away, but in essence he said, "Drop dead, Dad." He wanted no further relationship with his father, except his father's money to spend.

According to this parable, he left soon after he got the money: "Not long after that, the younger son got together all he had, set off for a distant country and there squandered his wealth in wild living" (Luke 15:13).

So his first step of independence from his father, the distancing, which he took even while still a member of his father's household, and the second step of leaving his father's house and heading for the distant country, were not far separated.

There in the distant country, the son abandoned all judgment and reason and restraint. He didn't budget his money. He didn't invest it. He certainly didn't work to earn more. He just spent it unthinkingly.

Occasionally one of his friends would ask about his family: "What's your father like?"

"Oh, he's stern, unbending, exacting. Really strict. Can't ever please him."

"What about your older brother?"

"He's a drag. Always out in the fields before sunup. Always trying to please the old man. Let's talk about something else."

This younger prodigal had too many friends—the wrong kind. And when he ran out of money, his friends left and things got hard there in the distant country. "After he had spent everything, there was a severe famine in that whole country, and he began to be in need" (verse 14).

This was a new experience. He was hungry for the first time in his life. He was ragged and tattered. And the friends he thought he had didn't know him now. So, he did what prodigals have done for centuries. He began trying to save himself from the mess he had gotten himself into. He went to work, hoping to get his act together and satisfy his immediate and urgent needs.

Gradually he came to the end of his meager resources. His money was gone. He had pawned his topcoat long ago. He had sold his suit and vest and even his shirt. Finally, Scripture says, "he came to his senses." He not only realized his needs, but he realized his own helplessness. That's what happened to him there in the pigpen. And when that happened, his attitude toward his father began to change.

He began to remember how his father treated his servants. His father was a far kinder master than the one he now worked for. The servants in his father's house had plenty to eat and decent clothes and a place to live. He looked around the pigpen with disgust. "My father's servants are better off than this," he told himself, and a plan began to form in his mind.

As he came to his senses, he also began to come to his father. He still underestimated his father's love and acceptance, but he no longer saw his father as a tyrant. And so he planned a speech. He would go back home and ask to be taken on as a servant. Who knows? Maybe his father would even give him special consideration.

Then he gave up trying to fix his own life. He didn't wait to save money for some new clothes or for a donkey to ride home. He immediately arose and headed for his father's house. And wonder of wonders, before he even got to the gate, his father came running to meet him. His father, with aching heart, had been yearning for his return, and when he saw him coming afar off, he ran to meet him. Love is of keen sight.

The son began his carefully rehearsed speech, but he never got a chance to finish it. He said, "I have sinned," and his father put his own robe around him to cover his shame. He said, "I am no longer worthy," and his father put a ring on his finger, reinstating him in the family. He had planned to ask for a servant's place, but he never had the chance, for his father put shoes on his feet—servants didn't wear shoes in those days. He was accepted and established fully as his father's son. And in place of the husks that the pigs had fed upon, he now feasted from the bounties of his father's table.

THE SECOND PRODIGAL

Meanwhile, the older son was in the field. When he came near the house, he heard music and dancing. So he called one of the servants and asked him what was going on. "Your brother has come," he replied, "and your father has killed the fattened calf because he has him back safe and sound."

The older brother became angry and refused to go in. So his father went out and pleaded with him. But he answered his father, "Look! All these years I've been slaving for you and never disobeyed your orders. Yet you never gave me even a young goat so I could celebrate with my friends. But when this son of yours who has squandered your property with prostitutes comes home, you kill the fattened calf for him!"

"My son," the father said, "you are always with me, and everything I have is yours. But we had to celebrate and be glad, because this brother of yours was dead and is alive again; he was lost and is found" (Luke 15:25-32).

Which prodigal son do you identify with? This father had not one, but two of them, didn't he? The second prodigal thought he had done well in keeping the commandments, for he says, "I've . . . never disobeyed your orders." But his obedience was a legal obedience only, and as such was worth nothing. The one who attempts to keep the commandments of God from a sense of obligation, merely because he is required to do so, will never enter into the joy of obedience. He does not obey. Obedience is a matter of the heart, not merely the outward actions. The elder brother gave evidence here that he was a prodigal at heart even though outwardly he was still in his father's house. He was in a distant country on the inside and hadn't even progressed as far as the pigpen!

The elder brother was a "good liver." But it isn't much fun being good in the way he was good. That kind of good living will put ulcers in your stomach and lines on your face, because badness held in check is not goodness and never will be. Sitting on a keg of dynamite that is about ready to explode is a terrible experience—more terrible the longer you sit there. And things finally exploded the day of the feast. All of the hostility the elder brother had held in came to the surface.

He had watched in silence for years as his father spent time looking down the road with his binoculars instead of looking at the good job this elder son was doing in the field. He had wanted his father to forget about his younger brother. In his mind, his younger brother was as good as dead—even when his father came out from the feast to reason with him, he referred to his brother contemptuously as "this son of yours" instead of "my brother."

But was the father more concerned for one of his two prodigal sons than for the other? No. As soon as he realized the distance the older son had put between them, he went out to meet him too. He didn't give up on the elder son, even though he was being unreasonable. The father loved both of his boys and did everything he could to reach both of them.

In the robe and the shoes and the ring and the feast the father had made provision for the younger son. And he made provision for the older son as well. Have you been a prodigal like the younger son? There is forgiveness and acceptance and the robe of Christ's righteousness waiting for you, and a place of fellowship at His table. Have you been a prodigal like the elder son? Hear the father's voice saying, "Everything I have is yours." His forgiveness and acceptance and robe of righteousness and the fellowship with Him at His table are for you too!

Won't you join in the feast provided? It doesn't matter which of the prodigal sons you have been imitating. Everything the Father has is yours, if you will accept it. The Father has come out to meet you. He invites you into His family today.

Chapter 10

The Rich Man and Lazarus

Jesus told some weird stories. Recently I discovered that I've already used all the good ones, so I've been trying to understand the hard ones. It's kind of exciting to find some good stuff in the hard ones and to discover that Jesus didn't really waste words, not even in the story of the rich man and Lazarus.

At first glance we wonder why He had to lay this one on us! I mean, who needs the story of the rich man and Lazarus, which makes the conditions in the afterlife even more complex? Didn't Jesus realize how confusing this story was going to be? What is He saying in Luke 16? I didn't really want to bring this story up, but there is something about the inner voice that keeps nagging and saying, "Go ahead, there must be someone out there who needs this."

Some people say that this story is a parable. The Bible doesn't say it is. Most often the parables begin with the words "He spoke a parable . . ." This story doesn't begin that way. But that doesn't really make a lot of difference—most everyone agrees that the story of the prodigal son is a parable, and it starts the same way this one does. When Jesus began the parable of the prodigal son He said, "There was a man who had two sons" (Luke 15:11), and He went straight to the story. And to begin the story of the rich man and Lazarus, He said, "There was a rich man . . ." (Luke 16:19).

What a way to begin! How would you like to have that on your tombstone? "He was rich." Big deal! Most of the time when we write an obituary or an epitaph, we say, "He was kind," or "She was generous," or something of that nature. But "He was rich"? That's a pretty sad obituary. That's about all that could be said about this man, because, apparently, that's about all he lived for.

The story reads:

> There was a rich man who was dressed in purple and fine linen and lived in luxury every day. At his gate was laid a beggar named Lazarus, covered with sores and longing to eat what fell from the rich man's table. Even the dogs came and licked his sores.
>
> The time came when the beggar died and the angels carried him to Abraham's side. The rich man also died and was buried. In hell, where he was in torment, he looked up and saw Abraham far away, with Lazarus by his side. So he called to him, "Father Abraham, have pity on me and send Lazarus to dip the tip of his finger in water and cool my tongue, because I am in agony in this fire."
>
> But Abraham replied, "Son, remember that in your lifetime you received your good things, while Lazarus received bad things, but now he is comforted here and you are in

agony. And besides all this, between us and you a great chasm has been fixed, so that those who want to go from here to you cannot, nor can anyone cross over from there to us."

He answered, "Then I beg you, father, send Lazarus to my father's house, for I have five brothers. Let him warn them, so that they will not also come to this place of torment."

Abraham replied, "They have Moses and the Prophets; let them listen to them."

"No, father Abraham," he said, "but if someone from the dead goes to them, they will repent."

He said to him, "If they do not listen to Moses and the Prophets, they will not be convinced even if someone rises from the dead" (Luke 16:19-31).

Well, what is the lesson? What is the key in this story, in this parable? Apparently Jesus was meeting the Jews on their own ground. It was, as it is today, a popular idea that people go to their reward at death. The Romans, according to some scholars, had a fable that was pretty much this story. Jesus adapted the story, which apparently was well known, to teach other truths.

How do we know that He was not teaching the state of the next life and the condition in the next world? Well, it doesn't take any thinking person long to come to a conclusion on this one. If this is not a parable—if Jesus was going straight into an actual, real-life experience, then it doesn't add up at all, because this story portrays heaven and hell within shouting distance. How would you like heaven and hell to be within shouting distance so you could call back and forth and you could see back and forth? A mother whose son is in hell could see him and hear him in torment, and he could plead for a cup of water from his mother, but she couldn't give it to him. This would turn heaven into hell for the mother. So, thinking people don't take this story and use it as a basis of their belief concerning the afterlife. It doesn't add up.

The context of Jesus' teaching here reveals several things He apparently meant the story to communicate. One is that riches do not guarantee an easy entrance into heaven—a concept that was a shocker in those days. A second is that there comes a time when a great gulf will be fixed. Apparently Jesus was doing some prophetic thinking here concerning the Jewish nation, the chosen people. And a third great lesson He was trying to teach was that we are not to look for magic and the sensational to get our attention. We have the prophets, and that is enough—if that doesn't do, nothing else will. This was proved among the people of His day. Let's look more deeply at some of these points.

RICHES ARE NO GUARANTEE

First of all, riches do not guarantee an easy entrance into heaven. The apostles were victims of this kind of thinking—that if you were rich, you had guaranteed entrance into the heavenly country. They even asked Jesus about it. Jesus went so far as to startle them by saying that a rich man can hardly get into the kingdom of heaven. He said that it is easier for a camel to go through the little gate in the walls of the city called the "needle's eye." In surprise, the disciples responded, "Well, who then can be saved?" They were surprised because it was the popular idea that if you were rich, then you were blessed of God, and if you were poor, then you were cursed of God. So, if a rich man couldn't get in, how could a poor person even think of approaching the heavenly country?

Jesus tried to straighten that out. He tried to straighten it out by His own life. As you recall, the apostle Paul said, "You know the grace of our Lord Jesus Christ, that though he was rich, yet for your sakes he became poor, so that you through his poverty might become rich" (2 Corinthians 8:9). Jesus became poor. How poor? The poorest of the poor—with hardly a place to lay His head, hardly a blanket with which to cover Himself at the foot of the Mount of Olives or in the Garden. The foxes and the birds of the air were better off than He was.

Jesus came to give surety to those who struggle and hope, to those who are in poverty, because if the poor people can make it, then anybody can make it. Jesus said, "Feed my sheep"; He didn't say, "Feed my giraffes." Someone else said, "Yes, feed the sheep, for whatever the sheep can get, the giraffes can get also if they get down low enough." Save the poor. If you can save the poor, then the rest can be saved if they get down low enough.

Jesus also said, "Blessed are the poor in spirit, for theirs is the kingdom of heaven" (Matthew 5:3). He identified with the poor and became a brother to them, to bring hope to the poor who thought they had no chance. He clothed the poor with dignity and held His head high as He demonstrated that heaven's door is open to every man, woman, and child.

Well, when we read about the rich man, I suppose most of us would say, "How can that apply to me? Money talks and the last thing it said to me was, 'Bye, Bye!' So, how can this part of the parable apply to me?" We forget that each one of us is rich in something, and there is a beggar lying at our door. You might not be rich in money, but you might be rich in intellectual giftedness. You might be the kind of person who breezes through school and through some profession while hardly cracking a book. And while you're off skiing during vacation times, your friends are pounding the books. They are the beggars lying at your gate.

You might be rich because someone loves you, and you forget about the grouchy old lady down the street whom the kids run away from. You know nothing of her life or why she is that way, and your rejection of her makes her even grumpier. She is the beggar lying at your door.

You might be rich in talent, like those who can sing or play musical instruments, and I would be the beggar lying at the gate. You might be rich in sanguine abilities and be extroverted and gregarious, while someone else is in nothing but pain in the crowd. That person is the beggar at your gate. Or you might be beautiful and you don't know what it is like for those who struggle because they don't think they are beautiful. They are the beggars at your gate. Every one of us is rich in something.

Sometime or another in life, most of us have also experienced what it's like to be the beggar at the gate. The bumps and bruises of life have left us frail and battered and beaten. We have experienced failure and have wondered if there's any hope. We have wished for a few crumbs that would fall from the capable people's table. So, somewhere along in the story you can find yourself. Jesus was trying to make it clear that just because you are rich and blessed doesn't mean you will be in heaven, and just because you are poor doesn't mean you won't. The reverse is also true, that just because you are rich doesn't mean you will go to hell, or just because you are poor doesn't mean you will go to heaven.

The truth of the matter is that Lazarus's name means "God has helped." Lazarus, apparently, had some respect and honor and dependence upon God. On the other hand, the rich man did not need God. He could depend upon himself and his riches. Self-sufficiency was his problem, which was also the problem of the religious people of his day.

Let's not say that the rich man was totally heartless. Let's face it, he allowed the beggar to stay at his gate. He didn't have him hauled off somewhere else. He didn't have the welfare department pick him up and get him out of sight. In fact, he may have even been involved in social activities and social movements for the improvement of the world. He might have even been chairman of the social-movement committee, although he probably sent one of the employees to serve in his place. He might have given huge sums to charity. But whenever a funeral train went by, he closed the blinds because he could not stand the thought of someday having to say "Bye, bye" to the things upon which he depended. He lived sumptuously. He dressed in linen and fine clothes until the end came.

I suppose some of us could say, "I like this story. It reminds me of the fairy tales of old where the bad guy gets it and the good guy succeeds, where the squaring of accounts takes place." If we find ourselves wallowing in that, we have missed the point of the story and perhaps have distorted the story. The question is, Am I willing to join Lazarus in this beautiful description, "God has helped," something that goes on the tombstone of the poor? God has helped; He is my hope.

NO LONGER CHOSEN

Jesus was also saying something about the chosen people, the chosen nation. As you know, Abraham had been given the promise, and the promise to the faithful had come down through the generations. Jesus came in that line. These people were chosen and blessed, there's no question about it. Their abilities, talents, and gifts have been a wonder to the nations everywhere, even to this very day. But they had walked away from God, and God had been patient with them century after century. They vacillated between idol worship, revival, idol worship, revival, Baal, God, Baal, on again, off again. This had continued down to the time of Jesus.

Then Jesus came—Jesus who was God, and they were too busy feeding sumptuously every day on their own self-sufficiency to notice that God was among them. Now they were on the verge of trading places with the Gentiles. As Jesus' ministry came to a close it was almost that time when the rich people would find themselves in torment and the poor beggars at their gates would find themselves in Abraham's bosom. The apostle Paul had something to say about it. Do you remember that Paul was a classic example of the nobles of that race, of that culture, of that group of people? But he accepted Jesus on the road to Damascus and began to preach the good news that has come down to our very day, that if we are Christ's, then we "are Abraham's seed, and heirs according to the promise" (Galatians 3:29). If you belong to Christ, then you are Abraham's seed. Thus, Abraham's bosom and Christ's bosom are the same in the story.

The rich man represented the Jewish nation, and Jesus apparently was bearing down heavily on this just as He did in stories like the one about the vineyard, in which the owner of the vineyard sent his servants to receive the fruit, and they were stoned and persecuted and treated spitefully. That story concludes with the owner sending his son and the tenants saying, "Let's kill the son." Jesus told these kinds of stories again and again to the chosen people of His day to remind them that they were on slippery ice, that they were about to make the biggest mistake of their lives. But they didn't hear.

There are many people today who take a great deal of interest in the end times and the Old Testament prophecies. Many books have been written about this subject. And many of those books say that the Hebrew nation is going to become very significant in the end; all the world's events will center on it. The big question is, however, will the Hebrew nation accept Jesus as God? Will they accept Jesus as their Messiah? For the Bible is clear that only those who accept Jesus will be in Abraham's bosom. And the amazing thing is that even though a whole nation walked away from God way back when, every individual in that nation has the same privilege that every individual around the world has, because God is no respecter of persons. It makes no difference what culture I come from—if I accept Jesus, I go to Abraham's bosom. If I am Christ's, then I am Abraham's seed and an heir according to the promise. Isn't that a wonderful blessing and a privilege? Paul was a champion of this great truth.

Is it going to happen? Well, one of the problems is that there is a great gulf fixed, as far as the nations are concerned. That is part of the story. What happened? Jesus came. He did His best to win the people who were the chosen people as a nation. They turned Him down. And one day He stood on the Mount of Olives and looked across to Golgotha, where He would be in just a few short hours. He began to weep, and He said, "O Jerusalem, Jerusalem, you who kill the prophets and stone those sent to you." And then He used mother hen language: "How often I have longed to gather your children together, as a hen gathers her chicks under her wings"—in the storm or other danger, next to her heart—"but you were not willing" (Matthew 23:37, 38).

Jesus wept and pled, and finally He had to say, speaking as God, "Look, your house is left to you desolate" (Matthew 23:38). The people of the nation were scattered worldwide, and hell began. The places were traded. And today the people of that culture can see the Gentiles taking the gospel everywhere in the world, to every nation, kindred, tongue, and people. Today the words that they said at Pilate's judgment hall are still haunting. You remember how Pilate stood before the people after he tried to release Jesus. He took a basin and washed his hands and said, "I am innocent of the blood of this just person." And they said, "His blood be on us and on our children!" (Matthew 27:24, 25, KJV). What a prayer that was, which has been answered! But still, any individual of any race and any culture is welcome into the bosom of Abraham, the bosom of Christ. How amazing is the love of God!

The poor beggar at the rich man's gate represented the Gentiles. He was with the dogs. The dogs were licking his sores, and he was hoping to get a few crumbs from the rich man's table.

Here is how Paul describes the advantages of the Jewish nation: "Theirs is the adoption as sons; theirs the divine glory, the covenants, the receiving of the law, the temple worship and the promises. Theirs are the patriarchs, and from them is traced the human ancestry of Christ, who is God over all, forever praised! Amen" (Romans 9:4, 5). Paul describes the advantages of the Jewish nation, the chosen people, in large terms. He even indicates that Jesus came in that lineage.

On the other hand, here is what he has to say concerning the Gentiles in comparison—the Gentiles represented by Lazarus by the gate, living with the dogs: "Remember that at that time you were separate from Christ, excluded from citizenship in Israel and foreigners to the covenants of the promise, without hope and without God in the world" (Ephesians 2:12). But now the Jews and the Gentiles were about to trade places. "Now in Christ Jesus you who once were far away have been brought near through the blood of Christ" (verse 13).

Jesus used the term "dogs" to apply to the Gentiles.

Jesus did?

Yes. You remember Matthew 15, the woman of Tyre and Sidon up there in Syro-Phoenicia. Jesus visited her on a divine appointment because He came to heal her daughter. And He tested the disciples, who believed that the Gentiles were dogs. The first thing He did was ignore the woman who pled for help. The disciples thought, *Well, He agrees with us. Let's get rid of her.* Then He said, "I didn't come to help you." The disciples thought, *Well, well, that's the way we think too. She's bothering us.* Then He said, "It is not right to take the children's bread and toss it to the dogs." To dogs!

He was trying to teach the disciples a lesson, which becomes obvious later on in the story because of the way Jesus treated this poor woman after He had tested the disciples. More than once Jesus indicated to the disciples and the people of His day the faultiness of their view of the Gentiles. The chosen people thought the Gentiles weren't worth much, but Jesus told the story of the Samaritan who poured oil and wine into the wounds of the man who had been beaten by the thieves and robbers. It was a Samaritan, a "dog," who had helped the poor person with his wounds. And in this story of the rich man and Lazarus, there is also something about the dogs that come and lick the poor man's wounds.

The other day I was raking rocks, which seem to grow in Arkansas. (This is my new profession now, raking rocks. When you build a house in the meadow, it sure messes up the meadow, and you end up having to spend the rest of your life raking rocks!) Well, into the yard came a Rottweiler dog. I got sweaty palms. I remembered the wife of the editor of *Signs of the Times,* who was attacked by pit bulls in Texas. They just about butchered her. I thought the Rottweilers were first cousins of pit bulls.

I had seen this dog and her husband, who was huge, checking out my place the other morning. When we yelled out the window and asked them to go home, they just looked at us. So, when I saw her approaching me, I got tight stomach muscles. Then I made the mistake of scratching her behind the ears, and she adopted me. She stayed the rest of the day. When I started my lawn mower, she attacked it. So I turned it off; I didn't want her to lose her feet. We became friends, and she brought me comfort because I thought she might speak a good word to her husband in my behalf. The dogs brought comfort to the poor man at the rich man's gate.

This story shows that Jesus came to place value upon the human soul. In the days of Christ there wasn't much value to the human being. It was like today in the ghettos and among the Mafia, if you please. In the days of Christ, slavery was everywhere. Historians tell us that a slave was hardly worth thinking twice about. When slaves were too old to work, they just stopped feeding them. And when they could hardly move any more, the owners would take them out to the garbage collectors to be picked up and hauled off to the local Gehenna. Jesus came into a world like that to show that the slaves and the poor are worth everything in heaven's sight. He came to show that if we could have giant scales and put the world, which weighs six sextillion tons, on one side and put one human being, the weakest of the weak, on the other side, the human being would tip the scale. Jesus came to be a brother to the poor and to prove how highly heaven regards every person. That includes you and me.

As you know, in the story the rich man dies and goes to hell. The beggar dies and goes to the bosom of Father Abraham. This expression is not just Old English language; it is modern as well. We say, "We are bosom friends." Well, that expression was around in Bible times too. It meant that the beggar, Lazarus, was close to Father Abraham, next to his heart. And the people of that day took a great deal of stock in being children of Abraham. The point is that instead of the rich man ending up there, it was the poor beggar who ended up there.

When I was a little child, I had an old book called *Sabbath Readings for the Home Circle.* That book contains a story about a rich man in Paris who would ride his carriage out into the country-side each day. One day as he was riding along, he heard people say that the richest man in Paris was going to die. He took some stock in the word of the prophet who said that. So, thinking he might be the richest man, he began worrying. He had the doctor come and stay by his bedside twenty-four hours a day. They took his temperature, and they watched his vital signs, but he didn't get sick. He didn't even cough. He was fine.

One day as he was out riding in the countryside, he saw a disturbance in the bushes. He got out of his carriage and pushed the bushes apart. There he found a poor peasant praying. The peasant's face was aglow as he looked toward heaven, thanking God for His many blessings and for His great kindness. A few days later the rich man found out that the richest man in Paris had died. To his surprise, it was the poor peasant who had died. He was the richest man in Paris. He was rich in faith.

LEARNING THE GEOGRAPHY OF HELL

Well, what is hell? I think raking rocks is close. The deeper you rake, the more rocks come up. I had this fantasy of digging so deep that I finally got to hell. The devil said, "Welcome." And I said, "Sorry, I've already been there!"

People try to get the geography of hell straight. Some say it is the inferno in the center of the earth. Others who read the

Bible say, "No, it is the earth." And still others say it's somewhere else.

What is hell? We have here something that is deeper than a fire of flame. It is a different kind of torment. Hell is the closed door. Hell is the realization that everything has been forfeited forever. Hell is finally understanding that there is no second chance. Forget reincarnation and all the rest of the maneuvers that people have made in the world's religions. Our destiny is decided in *this* life. And this is a great Bible teaching.

Someone said, "Hell is separation from God." No, the wicked would love to have separation from God. That would be heaven for them. It's more than separation from God. It is the sense of utter nothingness that comes apparently at the second death, at the time when the wicked realize that they've forfeited everything forever. This is the torment of hell.

Helmut Thielicke pictured a rich man who was in hell and from there looked at his own funeral. Often during his lifetime he had allowed himself to imagine in pleasant moments of vanity what a splendid affair it would be! There would be many charitable societies in the procession. And surely the best preacher in town would praise him to the skies, while the poor upon whom he had showered a thousand benefactions would be sobbing in their handkerchiefs, because, after all, he was involved in many social reforms. But now he was actually seeing his own funeral. He sees it however from the viewpoint of hell. And suddenly and mysteriously this alters the whole picture. It's all so oppressively different from the way it appeared to his fantasy.

True, it is a magnificent funeral, but it no longer pleases him. It only gives him pain because it is in such screaming contradiction to his real state. He hears the shovelful of earth come thumping down on his coffin and one of his best cronies saying, "He lived life for its own sake." And the rich man interjects, though nobody hears him, "I failed to live. I am in anguish." Then the second shovelful falls, and another voice says, "He loved the poor in the city." And the rich man wants to shriek, "Oh, if they only suspected what the truth is. I am in anguish." Then the minister, the popular and beloved abbey of society, casts the third shovelful. "He was so religious that he donated bells and windows and the seven-branched candlestick. Peace be to his ashes." And as the clods of earth come tumbling down on his coffin—or is it the rumbling of hell that he hears—he cries, "I am in anguish. I am in anguish!"

On the other hand, the rich man of Jesus' story had what appears to be a touch of love in the flames of hell. He calls across the abyss to the poor man in Abraham's bosom and to Abraham, and he says, "Please, I have five brothers. Please go to them from the dead. If someone came from the dead, they might believe and be spared the torment that I am in." And Abraham calls back and says, "They have Moses and the Prophets." And the rich man says, "No, but if someone came from the dead, then they would believe." And Abraham says, "No, if they won't believe Moses and the Prophets, they won't believe anything. Not even the spectacular or magic."

"Five brothers." There are Bible commentators who say here we have the five colors of the human race. We used to sing it, "red and yellow, black and white." They should have added brown. Red, yellow, black, white, and brown—the entire human race. And the rich man, with what looks like love, says, "Spare them."

Then comes this story's final challenge to you and to me: It is possible for us to fare sumptuously every day on Moses and the Prophets. Are you doing that? We don't have to lie by the gate of the rich man. We can fare sumptuously because of what has been provided. It also explains why Jesus was reluctant to do the spectacular; why He kept a low profile on many of His miracles. He knew that the spectacular doesn't change anybody.

What am I waiting for before I would begin to fare sumptuously on Moses and the Prophets? Am I waiting for some kind of fireworks in the sky? Am I waiting for something spectacular, for some magic show? The ironic thing was that someone was raised from the dead a few days after Jesus told this story. His name was Lazarus, of all things. And not only did they not accept Lazarus's resurrection, they wanted to put Jesus to death, the One who raised Lazarus, and Lazarus, for proving that Jesus was right. If I don't get my religion from the Bible, I will get it nowhere else. And the end-time showers of fireworks will make no difference.

There is no such thing as salvation by grace alone. It is always salvation by grace through faith. And faith is at the table where Jesus meets us morning by morning. If I turn a deaf ear to His call day by day, after a while a great gulf is fixed, and I have a hard time getting across that gulf. The Jewish nation finally committed the unpardonable sin and no longer heard the voice of the Holy Spirit.

I plead with you today and I plead with my own heart to join the poor beggar at the rich man's gate and to accept the name "God has helped" and all that comes with it. I want that. Do you?

Chapter 11

The Heavenly Pay Scale

It happened at a church-sponsored school situated in Brooklyn. The students were encouraged to become involved in what was called "progressive class work"—completing certain lists of activities and learning certain skills for each grade level. Those of us in the first grade had been studying hard all year to get our Busy Bee and Sunbeam pins and scarves. The older students had worked to become Friends and Comrades and Master Comrades. (This was before we were sensitive about Russian communism!)

And so the night of the investiture came, when we were to receive our awards. I looked at the table where the youth director had laid out all the certificates and pins and scarves, and I saw I was to receive a small green kerchief for my work. The older students were to receive larger kerchiefs with shiny plastic sliders, but we first- graders had to tie a knot in our scarves to keep them together!

I had studied hard for my award and felt rather disappointed at what I was getting in return. I remember smiling desperately at the youth director, hoping he would notice me and feel sorry for me and maybe give me one of those plastic sliders. But it didn't work. That evening I discovered the painful truth that in this world you work for what you get, and you get what you work for. And that's the way it is.

When the meeting was about over, someone had a bright idea. My father and uncle were evangelists, holding meetings in down-town New York City. Someone said, "Why, these preachers must have learned all these things that the Master Comrades know. Why don't we invest them right now—and their wives too?"

So my father and mother and uncle and aunt went forward and were invested as Master Comrades. And I knew good and well they hadn't even done the requirements for Busy Bees or Sunbeams! I was not the least bit happy about the honor given to my parents that night. I still loved my parents, you understand, but I wasn't at all sure about the youth director. In fact, I felt so deeply about the experience that it set back my interest in progressive class work by at least twenty years. I didn't realize until years later that Jesus told a story that was very similar to that investiture service.

The kingdom of heaven is like a landowner who went out early in the morning to hire men to work in his vine-yard. He agreed to pay them a denarius for the day and sent them into his vineyard.

About the third hour [9 A.M.] he went out and saw others standing in the marketplace doing nothing. He told them, "You also go and work in my vineyard, and I will pay you whatever is right." So they went. [Apparently they trusted him, for he didn't specify the amount of remuneration.]

He went out again about the sixth hour and the ninth hour [12 noon and 3 P.M.] and did the same thing. About the eleventh hour [5 P.M.] he went out and found still others standing around. He asked them, "Why have you been standing here all day long doing nothing?"

"Because no one has hired us," they answered.

He said to them, "You also go and work in my vineyard" (Matthew 20:1-7).

Well, one thing is sure. You're not going to earn much going to work at five in the afternoon, one hour before quitting time. But maybe they could at least fill their pockets with some grapes to take home for supper. And so they went willingly to the vineyard.

When evening came, the owner of the vineyard said to his foreman, "Call the workers and pay them their wages, beginning with the last ones hired and going on to the first."

The workers who were hired about the eleventh hour came and each received a denarius (verses 8, 9).

We may not be too impressed with the "denarius," or "penny," as it's called in the King James Version. Inflation has made pennies so worthless that people hardly bother to pick them up off the street anymore. But in Jesus' day, a penny was a day's wage. So, the workers who had been hired at the eleventh hour were astonished.

The workers who had been there all day were astonished too. Their hopes began to rise, and they could hardly wait for their turn to come to the paymaster's table.

So when those came who were hired first, they expected to receive more. But each one of them also received a denarius. When they received it, they began to grumble against the landowner. "These men who were hired last worked only one hour," they said, "and you have made them equal to us who have borne the burden of the work and the heat of the day."

But he answered one of them, "Friend, I am not being unfair to you. Didn't you agree to work for a denarius? Take your pay and go. I want to give the man who was hired last the same as I gave you. Don't I have the right to do what I want with my own money? Or are you envious because I am generous?"

So the last will be first, and the first will be last (verses 10-16).

Well, this is indeed a strange story, isn't it? We understand that the vineyard owner represents God, and that makes it even stranger. Yes, we can agree, it's lawful for Him to do what He pleases with His own. Since all things belong to Him, it's all right for Him to be generous. But why did He discriminate against the ones who had worked such long hours? If He wanted to give His gifts to those who didn't deserve it, why stop with the one-hour workers? Why not give everybody ten pennies or a hundred? It looks as if He was being generous to some and not to others. And that makes us uncomfortable.

THE PENNY

The secret to understanding this parable is found in what the penny represents. What are the wages that are paid to the workers for God? Are they given advantages and blessings here in this life? Are they given a mansion of gold or stars in their crown or a special place in the kingdom of heaven to come? And if this is the case, why wouldn't it be best to hold out until the last possible minute before joining God's service so as to experience His generosity instead of feeling shortchanged?

It's quite obvious that God operates on a different value system than we do. But since that's true, we'd better take advantage of the opportunity given us in this parable to understand a little more about His system. If we're unhappy with His method of payment now, we'll certainly be unhappy later too.

So, what is the reward? What is the penny? It is Jesus Himself! He can't give the twelve-hour workers more than the one-hour workers, because He can give neither more nor less than Himself. Why? Because in giving Himself, He gives all the riches of the universe.

When you've seen that, you realize that, in a sense, the twelve-hour workers received more than did the one-hour workers after all, for while the one-hour workers were standing idle in the marketplace, the twelve-hour workers were enjoying the privilege of a full day of fellowship and companionship with the owner of the vineyard.

If you think that the reward is heaven and perhaps more stars in your crown or a bigger mansion, you will be disappointed. But when you realize that the reward is Jesus and that heaven itself can offer nothing more, nothing greater, then your reward begins when you enter His service. Through Jesus we enter into rest, so for those working with Him, heaven begins here.

We respond to Jesus' invitation "Come, learn of Me," and in thus coming we begin the life eternal. Heaven is a ceaseless approaching to God through Christ. The longer we are in the heaven of bliss, the more and still more of glory will be opened to us; and the more we know of God, the more intense will be our happiness.

Matthew 19 tells us that one day Jesus met a rich, young ruler, who came running after Him, wanting to know what to do to enter into life. Jesus said, "Keep the commandments." He was trying to smoke him out of the woods. "Keep the commandments."

"I have."

"What about this one?"

"Uh oh. I'm in trouble." And the man went away sorrowful.

The disciples, who were standing by and watching, thought, *Here is a rich man who refuses to follow Jesus. He is going away sorrowful. That's too bad. But we've chosen to follow Jesus. Therefore we're right, and he's wrong.*

Peter, who was usually the spokesman, got his mouth working first and blurted out, "Too bad for him, Lord. He left. But what about us? We're following You. What will we get out of it?"

Peter was operating on our system of values, wasn't he? "What will we get?" I think that if I'd been Jesus, I would have said, "You disciples get out of my sight. Give me another twelve and let me start over again. After three years, you still haven't gotten the message."

Instead, Jesus met them where they were. "Jesus said to them, 'I tell you the truth, at the renewal of all things, when the Son of Man sits on his glorious throne, you who have followed me will also sit on twelve thrones, judging the twelve tribes of Israel' " (Matthew 19:28).

Can't you imagine how excited the disciples were about the good news of the reward they would receive for following Jesus!

But then Jesus went on and added something else: "And everyone who has left houses or brothers or sisters or father or mother or children or fields for my sake will receive a hundred times as much" (verse 29). Mark adds, ". . . in this present age . . . and in the age to come, eternal life" (Mark 10:30).

Since the reward is Jesus Himself, the reward begins here and now—a hundredfold. And the reward at the end of the day is simply a continuation of the experience already begun. The rewards *in* service are just as meaningful as the rewards *for* service. Fellowship with Jesus is the highest reward that can be given.

Those who are unwilling to stand all day idle and who are more interested in service and fellowship with Jesus than in the rewards that may be given will find in the end that the reward will be enough—more than enough.

Chapter 12

Jesus' Last Stand

General Custer said to his men, "I have good news and bad news for you."

They said, "What's the bad news?"

He said, "We're surrounded by Indians."

"What's the good news?"

"We won't be going back to South Dakota."

Well, the people who like to tell South Dakota stories smile and laugh and continue to tell them. But there was no one telling them that day. In fact, the only thing left from Custer's last stand is a memorial and memories.

Today there are all kinds of memorials, living memorials, to Jesus. That's because though He died, He was resurrected and went back to heaven. And He promised, "I will come back and take you to be with me that you also may be where I am" (John 14:3).

With that in mind, let's take a look at Matthew 23, one of the hardest-hitting chapters in the Bible. (I wonder what you would do

with this chapter if you came across it during your devotional time.)
We want to get the full flavor of Jesus' last stand:

> Jesus said to the crowds and to His disciples: "The teachers
> of the law and the Pharisees sit in Moses' seat. So you must
> obey them and do everything they tell you. But do not do
> what they do, for they do not practice what they preach. They
> tie up heavy loads and put them on men's shoulders, but
> they themselves are not willing to lift a finger to move them.
>
> "Everything they do is done for men to see: They make
> their phylacteries wide and the tassels on their garments
> long; they love the place of honor at banquets and the most
> important seats in the synagogues; they love to be greeted
> in the marketplaces and to have men call them 'Rabbi' "
> (Matthew 23:1-7).

Then Jesus gave instruction about that:

> The greatest among you will be your servant. For who-
> ever exalts himself will be humbled, and whoever humbles
> himself will be exalted.
>
> Woe to you, teachers of the law and Pharisees, you
> hypocrites! You shut the kingdom of heaven in men's faces.
> You yourselves do not enter, nor will you let those enter
> who are trying to.
>
> Woe to you, teachers of the law and Pharisees, you hypo-
> crites! You travel over land and sea to win a single convert,
> and when he becomes one, you make him twice as much a
> son of hell as you are. . . .
>
> Woe to you, teachers of the law and Pharisees, you hypo-
> crites! You give a tenth of your spices—mint, dill and cumin.

But you have neglected the more important matters of the law—justice, mercy and faithfulness. You should have practiced the latter, without neglecting the former. You blind guides! You strain out a gnat but swallow a camel.

Woe to you, teachers of the law and Pharisees, you hypocrites! You clean the outside of the cup and dish, but inside they are full of greed and self-indulgence. Blind Pharisee! First clean the inside of the cup and dish, and then the outside also will be clean.

Woe to you, teachers of the law and Pharisees, you hypocrites! You are like whitewashed tombs, which look beautiful on the outside but on the inside are full of dead men's bones and everything unclean. In the same way, on the outside you appear to people as righteous but on the inside you are full of hypocrisy and wickedness.

Woe to you, teachers of the law and Pharisees, you hypocrites! You build tombs for the prophets and decorate the graves of the righteous. And you say, "If we had lived in the days of our forefathers, we would not have taken part with them in shedding the blood of the prophets." So you testify against yourselves that you are the descendants of those who murdered the prophets. Fill up, then, the measure of the sin of your forefathers!

You snakes! You brood of vipers! How will you escape being condemned to hell? (verses 11-33)

And then we go to our knees for a glad time of prayer after reading our chapter for the day, right? It kind of makes you wonder if it would be similar to the priests in the days of Israel killing lambs all day and then coming in for family worship that night.

What is Jesus doing here—"hypocrites," "blind guides," "fools," "snakes and sons of snakes"? If I were to read this passage to you, you would probably hear the gravel in my voice, because that's about all I can produce when I read things like "snakes" and "sons of snakes" and "fools." But the interesting thing is that Jesus, we understand, had tears in His voice when He uttered His scathing rebukes. Try that. I dare you to try that tomorrow morning in front of the bathroom mirror. Try to say "snakes and sons of snakes" with tears in your voice.

Is there anything in this passage for us? The interesting thing is that this story took place just before Jesus' death, during His last week here on earth. This was His last moment, just before He left the temple forever—when He said, "Look, your house is left to you desolate" (Matthew 23:38). This was His last stand. Yet He did not lose. He went away a conqueror, even though He was weeping and saying, "O Jerusalem, Jerusalem . . ." (Matthew 23:37). Why did Jesus do this? Did He lose His temper finally? Was He letting them have it? Or if we had been there in the crowd, would we have seen another dimension in His body language, in His eyes filled with tears? And what can we learn from it today?

A BUNCH OF SICKIES

The truth of it is that He was looking at a bunch of "sickies." I guess that's the way we might say it today. Those people were sick. Their leaders were sick. They had a disease known as "mere morality." And today we are told that many who call themselves Christians are mere moralists—which means that many Christians are nothing more than external conformists. They do all the right things, but they do them for all the wrong reasons. External religion, Jesus pointed out again and again, is not enough. And the nature of the problem is clearly portrayed in these verses, where

He says, "You hypocrites! You clean the outside of the cup . . ." That isn't going to do it. "First clean the inside of the cup . . . , and then the outside also will be clean."

As my brother and I were growing up, we had an interesting form of kitchen economics going on when we washed the dishes: We took turns; he washed and I dried, then I washed and he dried. Whenever it was my brother's turn to dry, he took great delight in finding one little speck on a dish or a cup and throwing it back in the wash. But I got even the next time. We discovered one thing for sure: When we had scrubbed and scoured and worked on the inside of the pots and pans, the outside was automatically clean. And Jesus took off on that simple little illustration.

Can we place ourselves in these people's shoes? Our church was told a long time ago something very interesting: "The trials of the children of Israel, and their attitude just before the first coming of Christ, have been presented before me again and again to illustrate the position of the people of God in their experience before the second coming of Christ."[1] So, if we want to know what the people were like in the days of Jesus, all we have to do is look in the mirror. Ouch!

Here is something else that is shocking, from the book *The Great Controversy:* "There is a striking similarity between the Church of Rome and the Jewish Church at the time of Christ's first advent. While the Jews secretly trampled upon every principle of the law of God, they were outwardly rigorous in the observance of its precepts."[2]

We learn in mathematics that two things that are equal to the same thing are equal to each other. So, if there is a big similarity between Rome and the Jews at the time of Christ's first advent and a big similarity between the Jews at the time of Christ's first advent and us at the close of time, then there is a great similarity between us and Rome. And what is the crux of the problem? It is something that has plagued Christianity for a long time: mistaking good behavior for Christianity.

Now, it just so happens that when we focus on behavior in terms of our life, our theology, our evangelism, or whatever, we fill the church with strong people. Strong people can make it, because they can conform outwardly to the rules and regulations and standards of the church and what is expected of them. But the weak people soon leave and become "backsliders."

The problem is that the strong people in the church are also candidates for Pharisaism—judging all those who are below them in terms of their performance. This is what Jesus was talking about. Apparently it was important for Him to take the masks off the faces of the religious leaders in the presence of the multitude. Apparently He intended to help people understand, just before His death, that these leaders who looked good on the outside were rotten on the inside. And it was demonstrated only hours later, in fact, when they took Jesus to a lonely cross on a public hill.

So, when Jesus repeatedly called them hypocrites and fools and blind and snakes, He had a purpose in mind; He wasn't just venting His spleen, as they say. The masses were being led by sick people. And Jesus, on more than one occasion, said, "You need to get to the doctor." "It is not the healthy who need a doctor, but the sick. But go and learn what this means" (Matthew 9:12, 13).

Now, in Revelation 3, we are told that the church in existence shortly before Jesus returns is called Laodicea, and Laodicea is known for being lukewarm. What is "lukewarm" made of? It's made of hot and cold. But you can't go by the kitchen sink on that. It doesn't mean that we are hot on the left side and cold on the right side. You go to Matthew 23, and you find out that lukewarm is made up of hot on the outside and cold on the inside. That is what makes lukewarm. People who are apparently hot on the outside, but cold on the inside—doing all the right things for all the wrong reasons.

God uses the illustration to point out why He is sick to His stomach. He says, "Because you are lukewarm—neither hot nor cold—I am about to spit you out of my mouth" (Revelation 3:16). In other words, God is saying, "Lukewarm stuff makes Me want to throw up." Lukewarm is not acceptable to God. It never has been, and it wasn't on that day when Jesus left the temple for the last time. So He took a stand and pointed out the symptoms and diagnosed the disease of those sickies who stood before Him, the ones who had led the people to the point of rejecting the Messiah.

Let's take a look at our own hearts and get a diagnosis. How are we to diagnose the sickness? Well, first of all we need someone beside ourselves to do the diagnosing.

Years ago, when I was pastoring in California, I decided I wanted to get a glucose tolerance test for a member of my family, because I had heard about blood sugar and its effects. So I called the medical center and said, "I'd like to order a glucose tolerance test."

They said, "Who's your doctor?"

I said, "I beg your pardon?"

"Who's your doctor?"

"Oh, I need a doctor?"

"Yes."

They reminded me very quickly that I cannot diagnose myself, thank you. But I thought I was big enough to do it. Are we big enough to diagnose ourselves? Well, Paul says, "Examine yourselves . . ." (2 Corinthians 13:5). That's what he said, "Examine yourselves." And we often do that. We take a look at our behavior, how we failed or where we succeeded, and we begin to examine ourselves in that regard—a behavior-centered religion. But that's not what Paul said. He said, "Examine yourselves to see whether you are *in the faith.*" That is, examine yourselves to see whether you are in a trusting relationship with Jesus. Relational theology involves a person and the experience that we call faith. Or, in the setting of sickness and wellness, examine yourselves whether you are in touch with the doctor, whether you are under treatment—because you are sick.

THE GREAT DIAGNOSTICIAN

We are all born with a sickness called sin. It has self as its basis and self-centeredness as its big symptom. And then there is a Great Diagnostician. His initials are H. S. You've heard of Him, haven't you—the Holy Spirit? Jesus said, "When He comes, He will convict the world of guilt in regard to sin and righteousness and judgment: in regard to sin . . ." because they didn't do the right things or because they did bad things? No: "He will convict the world . . . in regard to sin *because men do not believe in me"* (John 16:8-10, emphasis supplied). Jesus said it: because they don't trust in Me. Relational theology. And this is what Jesus was constantly trying to point out to the religionists of His day—that the issue is knowing God and letting Him take care of your sickness and your problems.

After reading Matthew chapter 23, I could get all excited about letting the leaders of our church have it. I could perhaps think of certain leaders into whom I'd like to burn this point. But on second thought, when I point my finger at them, I have several fingers pointing back where I'd better look. I'm in danger of being in the same camp and not knowing it, because Laodiceans don't know it. That's the tragedy. Lukewarm people don't know it.

Let us take a look at some of the symptoms of the lukewarm people. First of all, these kinds of people "do not practice what they preach" (Matthew 23:3). Jesus tells us to go ahead and do what they say, but do not do what they do.

They are also a burden to others: "They tie up heavy loads and put them on men's shoulders" (verse 4). Perhaps you've seen a fanatic. A fanatic, of course, would be anyone who is more zealous than I am. Or a fanatic is one who has lost his purpose but doubled his efforts. A fanatic can only talk about one thing. And fanatics cram their religion down other people's throats. They are a burden. I've seen it. I've accumulated case histories. And if I look in the mirror, I have to realize that I have the same potential of doing the same thing.

These people do their works to be seen of men. "Everything they do is done for men to see" (verse 5). They want to be noticed. They want to be in the spotlight. They could stand on the street corners in those days with their scriptures wrapped around their heads and their wrists and pray. It's beyond me to imagine the average citizen of that day leaning against the storefront window and saying to his friends, "Look at these marvelous Pharisees on the corner praying. Aren't they wonderful?" I think I would have said, "Weird! They're weirdos." But the people had fallen into this blind-guide and blind-follower pattern. Somehow they continued to revere these leaders whom Jesus was talking about that day.

Jesus also said that these people hindered others from getting into the kingdom. They "shut the kingdom of heaven in men's faces" (verse 13). This is really tragic, because the kingdom that is spoken of here is not the kingdom of glory. They had a big misunderstanding, as you know. They expected the kingdom of glory when Jesus was here the first time. But at that time He came to present the kingdom of grace. We now live in the days of the kingdom of glory, when He will come soon with all power and majesty. But we will never see the kingdom of glory unless we experience the kingdom of grace—which means we will never enter the heavenly country unless we first enter a relationship with Jesus and let

Him, the Great Physician, deal with our sickness and bring His remedies. It is a terrible thing to keep other people from understanding the gospel.

Another symptom, a very interesting one: Jesus mentions that these external religionists prayed long prayers (see verse 14). Well, let's watch out for that one. The next time you hear someone praying a long prayer, you might remember Matthew 23. I hope they do too. Apparently these people are not up-to-date with their prayers in their closets, so they have to pray long and try to get caught up in front of everyone else. That's why while one elder in Charles H. Spurgeon's church prayed on and on, Spurgeon, the great preacher, got up and said, "Well, while our brother is finishing his prayer, let's sing hymn number 356."

These leaders were great on church growth. They would cross land and sea to make one convert. And then, Jesus said, "When he becomes one, you make him twice as much a son of hell as you are" (verse 15). So, they would bring in people and make them just like themselves—which means that if you preach an external religion, you will bring strong people in who are also victims of external religion. And Jesus was unmerciful in tearing this mask from these leaders on His last day in the synagogue.

On another occasion Jesus said, "I, when I am lifted up from the earth, will draw all men to myself" (John 12:32). He was speaking as God. If anyone else—any other human being—said that, we would have said there is something wrong with him. But Jesus is God, and He could say it: "I, if I am lifted up . . . will draw all unto me." These religious leaders had it all backwards. They said, "If we can draw all unto us, then we will be lifted up." You can do the same thing today. You can be good on church growth and you can advertise your successes in terms of numbers and draw all people unto you. But it is all a farce. Jesus spoke out strongly against this.

Inconsistency is another symptom of these lukewarm people (see verses 16-22). And they were great tithe payers (see verse 23). They would pay tithe of the smallest things. In fact, they were great Sabbath keepers. They wouldn't even lift a handkerchief that fell to the ground. They were great on health reform. They wouldn't eat a gnat that fell in the soup. And they were great on family worship. They were anxious to get back from the Cross in time for sundown worship, as you recall. But verse 23 also says they had no mercy, no faith, and no justice. Basically, they had no love. And we are faced with the danger of being in the same shoes. So, it is good for us to read hard-hitting words like these. It is not all bad.

What, then, is the challenge?

Well, if I'm in danger of being sick like the religious leaders and sick like the people who followed them, then I'd better find out where the treatment is. And here's where we get to the good part. Jesus said the work must begin on the inside and then work its way out: "First clean the inside of the cup and dish, and then the outside also will be clean" (verse 26). Beginning on the outside and trying to work inwardly has always failed and always will fail. Have you discovered that? I've discovered that. My track record reveals a lot of wasted time and effort from trying to work from the outside in. The modern approach to changing behavior, using behavior modification, "fake it until you make it," is nothing but sawdust in the presence of Jesus' counsel. Begin on the inside and that *will* take care of the outside.

HEART SURGERY NEEDED

Before we can seek a remedy, we have to admit that we are sick, admit that we need a doctor (see Matthew 9:12). Then we have to admit that we can do nothing about our condition (see John 15:5). Don't try to patch up your own circumstances and your own problems. Don't try to put Band-Aids on cancer. Get to the doctor. David understood this. In Psalm 51, the great repentance psalm, he said, "Against you, you only, have I sinned." And then he pled with God, "Create in me a pure heart, O God, and renew a steadfast spirit within me" (Psalm 51:4, 10). What he needed and what we need is heart surgery.

When we go to the Great Physician and He says, "You need heart surgery. You need a new heart!" now, that is scary. A few years ago it used to be even scarier. I went to see a man in Stanford Hospital who was going to experience a heart transplant. He was an atheist from England. One of the doctors in my church was on the team. He wanted me to go visit him. We talked for a little while. I said, "I suppose you understand the risk?"

"Oh, yes."

The risk was high in those early days. "But," he said, "I've decided that if I have to live one more day like I feel now, I am not interested in living another day. Bring on the risk."

They did. And he died. But it was a privilege to remind him, just before he died, that God loves atheists too. Only God knew why he was an atheist. And God looks not only at *what* we do, but at *why* we do it as well.

Heart surgery requires that I surrender to the surgeon. When you agree to go under the surgeon's knife, you have surrendered yourself, right? I suppose that's why I'm always in awe of surgeons. I go to the hospital and I watch the doctors going in and coming out. I say, "Wow! This has got to be awesome! To be willing to take the lives of people under your knife!" But people surrender to this. And surrender is the essence of Jesus' teaching.

The Great Physician has promised, "I will give you a new heart and put a new spirit in you" (Ezekiel 36:26). Will it take some blood transfusion in the process? Yes, it will. Is there enough to go around? Yes, there is. "There is a fountain filled with blood, drawn from Emmanuel's veins." Will it take some cleansing in the process? Yes. Has that been provided? Well, Scripture says, "If we walk in the light, as he is in the light, . . . the blood of Jesus, his Son, *purifies* us from all sin" (1 John 1:7, emphasis supplied). And, "If we confess our sins, he is faithful and just and will forgive us our sins and *purify* us from all unrighteousness" (1 John 1:9, emphasis supplied).

Can we trust the Great Physician? Can we trust the Surgeon? Can we admit our great need?

I used to want to be a medical missionary. When I went to college, I wanted to be a cowboy or a jazz drummer or a medical missionary. They weren't teaching the first two, so I tried for medicine. Then came cat lab and frog lab. One night the nurses showed a surgery film. The place was crowded. It was warm. I was standing. And I wasn't standing very long. When you get lightheaded and you stumble your way back to the dormitory, you say, "And I'm going to be a doctor?" So I got the victory over that.

One day, years later, Dr. Wareham invited me to watch an open-heart surgery at White Memorial Hospital in Southern California. I thought I'd probably faint again. But I got so absorbed in the surgery that I didn't have time to faint. I watched as the team did their work. They opened up the patient, an eighteen-year-old boy, and hooked him to the heart-lung machine. Then they opened up his heart. And there was the valve that had been restricted from birth.

Dr. Wareham just stood there while they did all that. Then it was his turn. He took the knife and began going with the heart beat, like a mechanic adjusting tappets on a Chevy. Then he just touched it, and it opened a little bit. And he touched it again, and it opened a little more. And he touched it a third time, and he was done. He put his knife down. He was finished. And they were glad to let him do it. Awesome! I got so fascinated by the surgery that I stayed the rest of the day. I watched a craniotomy. I watched a mastectomy. I saw someone else who was full of cancer; all they could do was sew him back up again.

The next day I went to visit the eighteen-year-old boy. He was red and ruddy now. I told him I'd seen parts of him that he'd never seen. And we talked. Awesome—to go in the hospital and to be under the surgeon's knife! I'm glad that Jesus knows what He's doing, aren't you? Can I trust Him? Will I surrender myself to His skillful hands? Will you?

Oh, and what about the cost? I get sick nowadays worrying about getting sick. Who's going to pay for it? The insurance? I can't even pay for the insurance. It makes a person want to move to Canada or England.

When it comes to the Great Physician, what is the cost? I have news for you. Good news. It costs nothing. And I have bad news for you. It costs everything. It costs nothing in terms of dollars and cents. But it costs everything in terms of surrender and saying, "God, I need You. I don't want to be like those white-washed tombs in the days of Jesus. I don't want to be like the blind followers that followed the blind leaders. I don't want to have to hear the words Jesus cried in His last stand—the words He cried just before He walked away: 'O Jerusalem, Jerusalem, . . . your house is left to you desolate.' " Yes, it costs nothing. But it costs everything.

I also have more good news for you: The prognosis is amazing. The prognosis is that, with the treatment, not only will I become well, but I will become more than well. I will be more than conqueror through Jesus, who loves me. And there's more interesting news: There is no discharge from this Doctor. I have to stay in touch with Him the rest of my days. And there is no discharge from the hospital. I have to stay in the hospital the rest of my days, going from patient to patient, telling them the good news of the Great Surgeon, the Great Physician.

This church is the hospital. It was called the inn in the days of the good Samaritan. You remember—the Samaritan took the wounded man to the inn, and he said, "Here, take care of him." He said this to the innkeeper. Now you are the innkeeper. " 'Look after him,' he said, 'and when I return' "—here you have the second coming of Christ—" 'when I return, I will reimburse you for any extra expense you may have' " (Luke 10:35).

This is the hospital for sinners, neighbor. And we stay in the hospital and we stay with the Physician. But without that—without the treatment and without staying with the Doctor, without staying in the hospital—the case is hopeless. It is terminal. It is called the second death.

What a wonderful privilege we've had, to look at a hard-hitting chapter, Jesus' Last Stand, and somehow to witness—amid the tears that choked Him up as He uttered His rebuke—to witness His friendly invitation to come and find help. Won't you come? Won't you accept Him into your heart and life? Won't you accept His transformation, His healing, the wellness that He has to give, and the invitation to stay with Him, to stay in the hospital until we see Him face to face?

1. Ellen G. White, *Selected Messages* (Hagerstown, Md.: Review and Herald, 1958), 1:406.
2. Ellen G. White, *The Great Controversy* (Nampa, Idaho: Pacific Press®, 1950), 568.

Chapter 13

The Ten Bridesmaids

Have you heard about the rich old man who lived in the mansion on the hill? He had ten children, but none of them had time for their father. They didn't come around anymore; they didn't even show up at their mother's funeral. They were too busy with their own concerns.

Then the rich old man had a heart attack. He was in the hospital about to die, and they all showed up. They made sure the bed was at the right angle. They made sure the oxygen was set OK. They made sure the pillow was fluffed just right. They stroked his brow. And they kept the dust off the will on the nightstand.

Corrupt motives! If you were the old man and had enough blood pumping across your cerebrum to allow you to think, you would see through that. What would you do with those ten children? You might hope that at least half of them were wise, even though most of them looked foolish.

We are going to have the opportunity to look at our own motives and where we are in our relationship with God as we notice another interesting story that Jesus told. It is found in Matthew 25:1-13:

> At that time the kingdom of heaven will be like ten virgins who took their lamps and went out to meet the bridegroom. Five of them were foolish and five were wise. The foolish ones took their lamps but did not take any oil with them. The wise, however, took oil in jars along with their lamps. The bridegroom was a long time in coming, and they all became drowsy and fell asleep.
>
> At midnight the cry rang out: "Here's the bridegroom! Come out to meet him!"
>
> Then all the virgins woke up and trimmed their lamps. The foolish ones said to the wise, "Give us some of your oil; our lamps are going out."
>
> "No," they replied, "there may not be enough for both us and you. Instead, go to those who sell oil and buy some for yourselves."
>
> But while they were on their way to buy the oil, the bridegroom arrived. The virgins who were ready went in with him to the wedding banquet. And the door was shut.
>
> Later the others also came. "Sir! Sir!" they said. "Open the door for us!"
>
> But he replied, "I tell you the truth, I don't know you." [Key phrase: "I don't know you."]
>
> Therefore keep watch, because you do not know the day or the hour.

What is Jesus telling us? We understand that this parable not only has meaning for the days when He first told it, but it also has particular significance for those of us who live today. Those of us who study the story realize that we are at the midnight of the world's history. We have increased technology, but we also have increased fear of what we're going to do with our technology. The world stands at the point of annihilation and self-destruction through economic disasters, natural disasters, and nuclear threats, and one of these days, the angels who hold the winds and who have their feet braced against the San Andreas Fault are going to let go, and all hell will break loose. Then we'll find out whether we have been wise or foolish. Then the big revelation will come. We'll discover whether we react with panic or devotion, whether we're running around with flared nostrils or whether we can relax and even sleep.

Well, how can we get a handle on the difference between the wise and the foolish so we know where we are? Please notice the key phrase in the story: "I don't know you." Wise people know God. Foolish people don't know God. Wise people pay attention to relationship theology, relationship experience. Foolish people hear but do nothing about it. They're all in the same church. Jesus wasn't talking about the world. The people the virgins represent are all in the same church. They all look alike, up to a certain point. But the wise people not only have a theory of righteousness by faith, they experience it as well. Foolish people have the theory of the gospel and might even rejoice in it, but they don't experience it. They're too busy with other things.

When Jesus lived on earth, He told the Samaritan woman by the well about the Spirit and the truth. You remember, He said that the day is going to come when people will worship in *Spirit* and in truth—not just in truth. Truth is not enough. Some of us grew up with certain phrases used in our subculture that went something like this: "We have the truth" and "We accepted the truth" and "We came into the truth." It became an old, worn-out, moth-eaten phrase because it left something out. The question is, When did we come into the *Spirit?* The question is not whether we have truth; it's whether the truth of the gospel has us and whether it has led us into a vital, personal relationship with Jesus. This is what the wise experience. The foolish had only a form of religion and went through the routines, but they were too busy to spend much time with the Father—the rich old Man on the hill.

We're talking about a Man who is really old. The last I heard, God has lived forever. That's pretty old. That's old enough to twist my brain all out of shape. Someone said that God created creatures with the power of choice who would love Him because He was lonesome. Well, He'd already been lonesome forever, so He must have had a change of personality; He suddenly became gregarious and sanguine and wanted people around. I began working on that and became all twisted out of shape. I can't figure all of this out.

But He's old and He's rich. He owns the cattle on a thousand hills and extensive mining assets. If He were hungry, He wouldn't tell you and He wouldn't tell me. He has mansions somewhere on the hilltop. But there's something He doesn't have: people. He wants people to take the place of the angels who fell. He wants people to repopulate heaven. He wants people to respond the day He comes and transfers the capital of the universe to this world. He said: " 'They will be mine,' says the Lord Almighty, 'in the day when I make up my treasured possession' " (Malachi 3:17). They will be mine—they that feared the Lord and spoke often one to another. But He wants people who love and respond to Him by choice and not by panic. He doesn't want people who suddenly wake up at midnight and begin beating their chests. So, Jesus tells this story.

WHAT THE SYMBOLS REPRESENT

In the story, the lamps represent the Word of God, the virgins represent a pure faith, the oil represents the Holy Spirit, and the light that comes from the oil through the lamps represents the light shining through God's people. When we think about this story, we often focus on the Holy Spirit. Someone wrote a book about this parable titled *The Golden Oil,* a book on the Holy Spirit. The interest there was on getting the Spirit. "Let's get the Spirit!" they say. And people use a number of ways to do that these days.

So, many are focusing on the Spirit, but the Spirit is uneasy, because the Spirit spends His time focusing on Jesus. The Spirit is never happier than when we focus on Jesus. When we are involved with Jesus, the Holy Spirit rejoices. Are we even supposed to get the Spirit, or is the Spirit supposed to get us? I'd like to propose that we don't even have to mention the Holy Spirit. When we get into the experience of the gospel and salvation by faith, when we become involved in relationship theology and are experiencing it, we are automatically talking about the Holy Spirit because He's the One who led us there. He's the One who makes it possible for you and me to be in communion with Jesus day by day. The Holy Spirit is in the middle of it all. And it is possible that preoccupation with the Holy Spirit would lead us down the wrong path, as it has happened to others. Please, let's focus on Jesus—where the Holy Spirit Himself focuses. After all, it's not might nor power, but the Holy Spirit that makes the difference—the Holy Spirit, who gets us to focus on Jesus. It isn't by my own might that I overcome my problems. It isn't by my own might and self-discipline and will that I obey. It isn't by my own might and power that I become victorious in the end time. It's only the Spirit, who leads us to look to Jesus. And it is not by power—political power or denominational power or any kind of power—that we can try and finish the work of the gospel. It's only by the Holy Spirit.

Another symptom that identifies the foolish bridesmaids: They had their eyes on the clock, and they got tired of waiting. Ironically, here is a blow to Adventism: It was the *foolish* bridesmaids who thought Jesus was coming back right away. It's the *foolish* people who said, "He's coming back tomorrow. I don't need extra oil." It's the *foolish* people who did not prepare for a long delay. Very interesting!

Perhaps, like me, you have grown up in a subculture in which people talked about it all happening tomorrow. That was true just recently with the magic year 2000 and then again with 9/11 and the Iraqi War. But "way back," centuries ago, people were talking about the end of the world. Mother Shipton, some sort of prophetess from England in the 1400s, wrote in poetic form about the end of the world. She described our world in detail and said that Jesus would come and the world would end in 1991. Well, the last I heard, we'd passed that date.

Then the jubilee people came along and said that it was going to happen by 1994. We passed that date. There are other time-setters who have continued to get us excited. The truth is, the wise people prepare for a long delay. While the foolish people have their eyes on the clock, the wise people have their eyes on the Bridegroom, whenever He should come. The foolish people don't know God; the wise people do. The foolish people have no time for studying the character of Christ or for communion with heaven. The wise people do.

Suddenly, while they are all sleeping—which is another enigma—the call is heard, "Here's the bridegroom!" A crisis! It's midnight. It's the darkest hour. They wake up. And right here we are faced with the painful realization that crises do not change us. Crises never change anyone. They only reveal what we already are. It makes no difference whether the crisis is cancer or death or an earthquake—all a crisis does is to reveal what you already are.

When trouble strikes one group of people, they say "Where is God when you need Him? Something's wrong with God!" They blame God. They are foolish people. But the wise people say, "The Lord gave, and the Lord took away. Blessed be the name of the Lord." They find this out when the crisis hits. If there is time after the crisis to change, people can change, and often they have as they've had time to think. But they do not change *during* the crisis. In fact, a crisis will usually increase people's momentum in the direction they're already going—as it did with Peter, who ran off and left Jesus in the Garden. When he finally showed up at the fireside and the bystanders pointed the finger at him, he added cursing to having forsaken Jesus, increasing the momentum in the direction he was already going.

In this story about the virgins, Jesus is apparently trying to help us do some serious thinking. He's trying to help us realize that while we still have time, while the door is still open, while we still can get it together, it is worthwhile to find out whether we are among the wise or among the foolish.

People sometimes get into the crisis of love. Have you ever heard of it? Have you ever been there? People fall in love, and they can't think anymore. They come into the church office, and they say, "What should I do? I'm in love with someone not of my faith, or someone of no faith, but he's a nice person. I'm in love." And I say,

"Too bad! Too late to think now, isn't it?" It's too late to think. You should have thought *before* you fell in love. So, it's better to do your homework before the crisis comes, whether it's love or the end of the world. And think carefully. This is what Jesus is trying to get us to do.

So, let's say, all of a sudden tragedy hits and I'm a victim of the theology of despair: Every time someone in my family has a sickness, we have a big revival; every time someone in my family gets run over by a car, everyone else gets re-baptized—a theology of despair. That's the way it is. We operate that way.

Now the devil enters the picture, and you know what the devil does when we panic and try to join the wise in a moment of crisis. He's done it before and will continue to do it. He beats us over the head with our corrupt motives. He's a master at this.

So, the devil comes along, beats us over the head, and says, "Ha, look at your rotten motives. Do you think God will accept you now? Why don't you look at how rotten you are? All you want is the will on the nightstand. That's why you're stroking your Father's brow." And he tries to discourage people who come with corrupt motives.

I'd like to remind you, neighbor, that most of us came to Christ with corrupt motives to begin with. We're hardly capable of anything else. By the "heaven to win, hell to shun" approach, someone gets our attention. But God will use any motive He can to get us started. He will even use corrupt motives to get us off the springboard into the pool of His love. He often has. So, let's not let the devil beat us over the head with our bad motives. If we come to Jesus, He will change our motives. Perhaps that's the only way they'll ever be changed.

Another interesting point in this story is that *all* these bridesmaids slumbered and slept. How do you explain that? It seems like the wise ones would stay wide awake and keep their lamps trimmed and burning, that they would be foolish to go to sleep. Right here we have a little bit of an explanation that some of us have appreciated. I'll never forget what a relief it was to come across this theme, the comparison between the Exodus and the Advent people. You remember that the Exodus people left Egypt and headed for the Promised Land. They were supposed to be in the Promised Land long before they got there. They faltered on the borders for years because of the lack of faith of those twenty years old and upward. All the younger ones wandered in the wilderness with their faithless fathers for forty years. God answered the prayers of the older people, who, you remember, had prayed, "Would God we had died in the wilderness." The younger folk wandered in the wilderness for reasons beyond their control.

The history of the Christian church and the history of our own subculture reveal a similar pattern. We're told our forefathers came up to the borders of the Promised Land decades ago. Then, because of their choices, we went back into the wilderness to wander. Historians in our own subculture have indicated that we've wandered in the wilderness. Then we heard, over the radio, the voice of one crying in the wilderness of these modern days, "Prepare ye the way of the Lord."

But we have wandered. Jesus has been lifted up on occasion. But we wandered. And the wandering was the result of behavior-centered theology instead of relationship-centered theology. We've focused on the law instead of on the Lord. We've focused on the end times instead of on the Bridegroom. We've focused on the signs of the times instead of on the heavenly kingdom. Then there comes an awakening, and those who have slumbered and slept for reasons beyond their control have the fulfillment of Psalm 126, a very interesting psalm:

When the Lord brought back the captives to Zion, we were like men who dreamed. Our mouths were filled with laughter, our tongues with songs of joy. Then it was said among the nations, "The Lord has done great things for them." The Lord has done great things for us, and we are filled with joy. Restore our fortunes, O Lord, like streams in the Negev (Psalm 126:1-4).

There comes a time when we wake up as from a dream. "Behold the bridegroom cometh!" We wake up and we say, "Why didn't someone tell us that Jesus always accepts us just as we are? We don't have to change our lives in order to come to Jesus. We come just as we are. He changes us. Why didn't someone tell us that?" We cry out, "Why didn't someone tell us that sin isn't what we usually describe as sin; it's living life apart from God? Why didn't someone tell us that when Hebrews 12:4 says, 'In your struggle against sin, you have not yet resisted to the point of shedding your blood,' it is talking about our struggle against *living life apart from God?* Why didn't someone tell us, 'He who overcomes [the sin of living life apart from God] will . . . be dressed in white' (Revelation 3:5)?

"Why didn't someone tell us that the *wise* bridesmaids are those who *know God,* and that this is the bottom line, and that all of our work and all of our day should revolve around that factor? Why didn't someone tell us that the gospel offers a doable? God doesn't expect us to never sin again; we will continue to fall and fail. But God asks us to respond to His knock at our heart's door for communion and fellowship and relationship with Him. Why didn't someone tell us?" We wake up as from a dream.

According to the story, when everyone woke up, they were *all* surprised. When the "Behold the bridegroom cometh" cry was heard, they were all surprised. It makes no difference whether I think it is 1991 or 1994 or 2000; according to the story, when the cry is finally heard, everyone is going to be surprised—the foolish *and the wise.* The church might be planning their greatest missionary advance when it happens. It will be a big surprise.

THERE'S BEEN NO DELAY

Some people say the Lord has delayed His coming. No, He hasn't. I read one day from someone more inspired than I am, "Like the stars in their appointed pathways through space, God's plans know no haste and no delay." The last I heard the plan for Jesus to come is one of His greatest plans. It will know no delay. It will be right on time. What time? Not the clock, but the time when the world comes to the point of self-destruction. That's when it happens. The God of love, who would not close the earth's history down before then because He wants to give you and me one more chance, will finally say, "Well, I guess there's no point in waiting any longer."

At this point in the story they all wake up. The foolish say, "Give us some oil." The wise answer, "No."

Selfish? It seems that if the wise were Christians, they would say, "Take it all. You can have the oil."

But they can't share their oil. Why? Because oil isn't transferable. The Christian life isn't transferable. That's what we're talking about here. No one can have a Christian life for another person. God has no grandchildren—only sons and daughters. I can't go to heaven by getting the oil from father or mother or preacher or neighbor or teacher. It is all one-to-one with God. This is integral to the story. They do not share their oil because you *cannot* give oil to another.

One of these days, according to Amos, people will be going from sea to sea and from coast to coast beating their chests and crying out in fear and beating down the doors of the righteous and saying, "Help me! I need something." But it'll be too late. They operate on panic instead of devotion. They watch the clock instead of the Bridegroom. They are more interested in the end times than they are in relationship with Jesus.

I'd like to remind you, neighbor, that the last I heard, the door of probation is still open, that we haven't come to the midnight hour quite yet, even though we're close. We can still wake up and move from being foolish to being wise. It's not that complicated. All we have to do is to take time to get acquainted with Jesus. That's what it's all about. It is making time with Jesus more important than football or TV or church work or anything else, so that everything slopes down from that relationship with Jesus. That's how we come to be numbered among the wise.

"Oh," someone says, "but you scared me, and now I'm going to come with a rotten motive."

That's OK. Welcome to the rotten-motive club. May I remind you of the prodigal son? He left the pigpen and headed toward the father's house because of his overwhelming love for his father—right? No, he left the pigpen and headed home because he was hungry, because he was naked, because he had no roof over his head.

Now, look at the father back home. Who does he represent? God—the rich man on the hill. And the last we heard, He understands our motives. He sees into our heart. He knew what was driving this prodigal son. How did the father treat the prodigal son? Did he put his binoculars down and go down the road saying, "Hey, wait a minute. Why are you coming back? Tell me. I think I have a good idea why you're coming back, you selfish son. You want some sandals on your feet. You want some clothes on your back, that's why. Why don't you go back to the pigpen?"

No, this father, with all of his insight into his son's heart, said, "Welcome home! Bring the shoes. Bring the garment. Strike up the band. Put on the feast. Have a party. This, my son, was dead and is alive."

The son came home with self-centered motives. But the only way you can change your motives is to have a loving father. And when you're treated like a son or daughter, then you'll begin acting like a son or daughter. You know, this son who'd thought that his father was a terrible slave driver from yesteryear must have gotten up the morning after the party and said, "Dad, can I help you out in the back forty? Do you need any fences fixed? Anything I can do on the farm?" Yes, because love begets love. It has happened again and again. Bad motives? Let God change your motives.

Back to the man with the ten children at the hospital bedside, what does he do? He looks at them and says, regardless of their motives, "How wonderful to have you here. Please come close. Let me give you a hug. I've missed you so much." And he puts his arms around them. This has to result in one of two things, either they're so wretched that they say, "Ha! We really pulled the wool over his eyes. Now, let's get to the will and divide it." Or they can fall down and bang their heads on the floor and say, "What is wrong with me! All the neglected phone calls and letters, and the holidays I could have been here. All the times I could have brought comfort and joy to his heart and didn't—and he still loves me! Please, Father, forgive me." I'd like to be among the wise ones. Wouldn't you?

There comes a time when it's all over for the foolish. That's part of the story too.

> Saddest of all words that ever fell on mortal ear are those words of doom, "I know you not." The fellowship of the Spirit, which you have slighted, could alone make you one with the joyous throng at the marriage feast. In that scene you cannot participate. Its light would fall on blinded eyes, its melody upon deaf ears. Its love and joy could awake no chord of gladness in the world-benumbed heart. You are shut out from heaven by your own unfitness for its companionship.[1]

God leaves the foolish out because He loves them. They would not be happy with Him. On the other hand, to the wise, to His faithful followers, Christ has been a daily companion and a familiar friend. They have lived in constant communion with Him, and heaven will be simply more—much more—of the same. That can be your choice and my choice today.

---

1. Ellen G. White, *Christ's Object Lessons* (Nampa, Idaho: Pacific Press®, 1952), 413.

Other books by Morris Venden:

Nothing to Fear

Devotions intended to prepare Christians for the end times and to deliver them from unnecessary fear. In classic Venden style, this beloved author gives us daily food for thought on topics such as, "How to Be Ready," "Revival and Reformation," "The Shaking Time," "Latter Rain Preparation," "Wrestling with God," and 15 others.

0-8163-1695-3. Paperback. US$9.99, Can$14.99.

How Jesus Treated People

A look at how Jesus treated the many different types of people He encountered, with encouragement for us to follow His example.

0-8163-0621-4. Paperback. US$9.99, Can$14.99.

How to Know God's Will in Your Life

Learn how much weight you can give to the advice of others, how to understand what you find in God's Word, and how important your feelings are in the decision process.

0-8163-0719-9. Paperback. US$8.99, Can$13.49.

Modern Parables

Through the years, Pastor Venden has used parables to help bring heaven a little closer to earth. He's now compiled the best-loved parables from his many sermons into one book.

0-8163-1196-X. Paperback. US$10.99, Can$16.49.

Order from your ABC by calling **1-800-765-6955**, or get online and shop our virtual store at www.AdventistBookCenter.com.
- Read a chapter from your favorite book
- Order online
- Sign up for email notices on new products